Finger Trigger Bullet Gun

a play by Nenad Prokić

for Stan's Cafe

translated by Mirka Jankovic

ISBN 978-1-913185-05-3

Published by Stan's Cafe
Birmingham, UK
2020

www.stanscafe.co.uk

Finger Trigger Bullet Gun © Nenad Prokić 2014
Translation © Mirka Jankovic 2014
Photos © Graeme Braidwood 2014
Publication © Stan's Cafe 2020

Contents:

Synopsis	4
Finger Trigger Bullet Gun (English)	5
Finger Trigger Bullet Gun (Serb)	35
Bonus Material	
Programme for Novi Sad	66
Blog post for The Guardian	68
Nenad's challenge	70
Nenad's answers	72

Synopsis

Prologue
In London two men, an Optimist and a Grump watch the funeral of Edward VII, they speculate as to whether there will be a war. Both men are killed on the battlefield.

Berlin 1
Kaiser Wilhelm, his Chief of Staff and Grand Admiral plot the elements that need to be put in place for Germany to start a successful war in Europe and extend their empire.

Vienna 1
Emperor Franz Joseph of Austria, his son Franz Ferdinand and Foreign Minister Count Berthold discuss the possibilities of a 'preventative war'.

Belgrade 1
Crown Prince Alexander Karadjordjevich tries to rein in Dragutin Apis and Vojislav Tankosich, members of the Black Hand secret military group, who are keen to start a war of their own.

Berlin 2
The Kaiser is ready for and enthusiastic about the war that is to come.

Vienna 2
Franz Ferdinand leaves for Sarajevo, little suspecting he is a sacrifice served up to justify a war of revenge.

Belgrade 2
Alexander's attempt to warn Franz Ferdinand has failed and his colleagues are ready for the war that is to come.

Sarajevo
Gravilo Princip assassinates Arch Duke Ferdinand.

Anywhere in Europe
The war starts.

Finale – London 2
The Grump explains to The Optimist why the Great War was not 'The War to End All Wars'.

Finger Trigger Bullet Gun

A.D. 2014

To Karl Kraus

Prologue

Graeme Streets of London. Funeral of Edward VII, 20 May 1910. A coffin glides by.

Optimist Our poor king! Ever since he fainted so suddenly in Berlin last year, I never stopped worrying about his health. Ah, tempi passati, you know it, nemo propheta in sua patria and all roads lead to Rome!

Grump Bronchitis. Never less than twenty cigars every day. Not a laughing matter that.

Optimist Our poor king! It is said that he died after several consecutive heart attacks. He suffered a lot, our poor king. When the Prince of Wales told him that his horse Witch of the Air had won in Kempton Park that afternoon, he just said: "Yes, I have heard of it. I am very glad". Those were his last words. He died fifteen minutes later. A feeling heart must show sympathy. Look, nine crowned heads in the procession, five crown

	princes, seven queens...
Grump	Yes! You think there will be no drama to follow this beautiful overture?
Optimist	Excuse me? Can you still deny it? You're so grumpy! Rumours are spreading that rumours are spreading! That's all there is to it!
Grump	The price of blood has fallen; the price of meat has risen.
Optimist	But they are all one big family, all nephews and uncles! They are the salt of the earth and the light of the world! The deceased was the brother of the mother of The Kaiser and he's here, don't you see him? There he goes in the uniform of a British field marshal! The widow's brothers are the kings of Denmark and Greece; the Russian court is affiliated too, and so are the Balkan royal houses...
Grump	And this will not stop them from being at each other's throats come tomorrow! There are stories behind stories there. You don't want to see that in the way The Kaiser is treated. Germany keeps testing its wish to be respected and appreciated.
Optimist	But, finally, there are some ideals! And some solidarity, in death at least! Does it not mean that evil is on its way out?
Grump	Evil advances the best in the footsteps of ideals. And behind the idea of sham solidarity.
Optimist	But – idea offers the possibility of cure!
Grump	One can die for the idea without ever healing. One does not die for the idea but on it. One dies for the idea even when there is none. One dies of it without even knowing it.
Optimist	Very droll. You are such a grump!
Grump	I am, though you must admit that you are an optimist!
Optimist	But look! What an idyllic picture!
Grump	And the last picture of the European idyll, probably.
Optimist	Stop it, for heaven's sake, at this hour at least, stop it! Look at this ball of harmony! The Uncle of Europe has died and there they are: King George V, Frederick VII of Denmark, Haakon VII of Norway, Alfonso XIII of Spain, Manuel II of Portugal, Albert I of Belgium, Ferdinand I of Bulgaria, Wilhelm II of Germany and Prussia, crown princes; there's Archduke Ferdinand of Austria and

	Alexander of Serbia; there's Maria Fiodorovna, the widow of the late Emperor of All the Russias; a relative of the Emperor of Japan has come, the former American President Theodore Roosevelt, a Chinese prince... Salt of the earth and light of the world!
Grump	But yet if the salt loses its saltiness, how can it be made salty again?
Optimist	Hush! Look at the wench, pretty, isn't she?
Grump	Stop it, she's a prostitute!

- - - - -

Grump	Here I am, standing in God's palm. The British Fourth Army on the Somme, Battle of Fromelles, 19 July 1916. I don't know why on earth I peeked over the half-demolished wall that morning. I heard nothing, but that nothing came from the left. It did not hurt. Gray clouds were above, Optimist. And then, I guess, I died.
Optimist	Here I am, standing in God's palm. I was killed five days before you, Grump. British Expeditionary Force, Bazentin Ridge. That morning I could not stop vomiting. All those spilled bowels! And then it happened. Just happened. Oh well, doesn't matter.
Grump	The storm broke out. It was a wild night. God's image has been destroyed.
Optimist	In the end death gives birth to dance. Hatred gives birth to a joke. Poverty gives birth to fraud. So, what is it then?
Grump	So, what is it then? *[Blackout]*

Berlin 1

Jack	Kaiser Wilhelm II, the last German Emperor and King of Prussia
Graeme	Helmuth Johann Ludwig von Moltke, Chief of the German General Staff
Gerard	Alfred von Tirpitz, Grand Admiral, Secretary of State of the German Naval Office
Gareth	Stadtschloss in Berlin. Branches behind large windows sway in the strong wind.
Moltke	Most grateful for the audience, Your Majesty! At your service, Your Majesty! We are ready! The sooner the war begins the better for us! We must fight now for what we want to achieve! Conquest becomes the law of necessity. A successful state knows how to start a war at the best moment for itself. France must be trampled so thoroughly that it never stands in our way again.
Wilhelm	The British are completely indifferent to the German struggle for survival. They side with the Slavs and Romanics who are blinded by their feeling of inferiority.

	They have been making plans with France for years. Russia will support Serbia and it is evidently doing so already. The monarchs of Europe throughout the years of my reign never paid any attention to my words, that for us and our allies the existing status quo is untenable! They never turned an ear! They will show more respect shortly, with our big navy standing behind my words. German War – that will be the name of the next war! For, mind you, war is not a random accident! Germany will no more add to its collection of insults! It will respond with an iron fist and flashes of the sword! I remind you that it will be a war we did not want, a war that was imposed on us.
Moltke	We shall make mincemeat of the Russians and the Serbs!
Wilhelm	Forget Serbia, Moltke; it's a second-grade front!
Moltke	We are ready. Demolishing the Belgian neutrality – that should be the first step as has been clear for a long time. Tsar Nicholas II is very weak and that has also been clear for a long time. We are ready and the others are not. We shall not wait for the Russians to modernise their troops and finish the railway they are building towards our territories.
Tirpitz	We are not ready.
	[Silence]
Tirpitz	The big fight needs to be postponed for a while. We must build the submarine base on Heligoland and widen the Kiel Canal. Without that, we lose the war.
	[Silence]
Moltke	How long would it take, Admiral?
Tirpitz	A year and a half.
	[Silence]
Moltke	We go to war in 1914 then.
Wilhelm	We have to come up with an alibi, something like a trigger for the war. The Balkans would be the best. Be careful, what we need is a truly exceptional provocation. To sow discord a little wouldn't be bad, it wouldn't hurt; it is high time.
	[He goes to the window and watches the branches in the wind]
Wilhelm	Get the navy ready for a conflict with Russia, and Britain too if it proves necessary. Start a campaign in the press

that Germany must side with Austria-Hungary in case of an intervention. Stocks for the troops need to be prepared. Set up the mobilisation committee. Gold reserves, bank deposits and shares to be returned to Germany. Activate the old officer personnel. Order all highly-ranking army men to repatriate their foreign private accounts. Make the mobilisation plan for the eastern front. Neutralise boneless individuals who advocate peace. I shall notify all our ambassadors that a war is likely to break out within a few years. And to the two of you I say: war in 1914. A year and a half from now. The German war. The struggle for our place in the sun! We, the Germans, who still have our ideals, shall wage a holy defensive war and the result of that war can only be peace. Peace that will bring us the expansion of our borders eastward and westward and in overseas lands where German world politics must have the main say. And then, after the war, come winter, I shall be able to get to the Riviera at long last. Salty air does my lungs much good. It seems the wind is blowing.
[Kaiser extends his right hand. Moltke and Tirpitz kiss it]

Moltke   Your Majesty is no longer God's instrument; God is an instrument of Your Majesty!

Wilhelm   Ha! That was a good one!
[Blackout]

Vienna 1

Gareth	Franz Ferdinand of Austria, Archduke of Austria-Este, Austro-Hungarian and Royal Prince of Hungary
Graeme	Count Leopold Berthold, Anton Johann Sigismund Josef Korsinus Ferdinand, Foreign Minister of Austria and former Ambassador to Russia
Gerard	Franz Joseph I of Austria, Emperor of Austria and Apostolic King of Hungary
Jack	Hofburg, Vienna. Winter 1913. Light snow falls on the city.
Berthold	Most grateful for the audience, Your Majesty. At your service, Your Majesty! May I respectfully report that this year we have to create a new state: Albania! Serbia must not gain access to the sea and at no cost may they create a joint state of the South Slavs. There are too many Slavs in our state already, more than a half of

	the population! Yet another big state of theirs in our neighbourhood is the last thing we need! In the German part of the empire, nota bene, the Germans make up only thirty-three per cent of the population! Our politics in the Balkans must not become an illusion after this Balkan War. The Russians must be stopped. Enough inflammable matter has been piled up to trigger an explosion under the most favourable conditions and in its flash Russia will be invited to celebrate the moment when it straightened up again.
F Ferdinand	I do not like the Serbs. I do not need a single Serbian plum. They are a people of conspirators. But the empire needs to be reorganised within. The Slavic element should be granted the statehood such as the Hungarians already have. Trialism could be a solution.
Berthold	Viennese militarists will send you packing if you say this aloud.
Franz Joseph	Conrad must be stopped! The Chief of the General Staff in Austria must forget his warmongering fever. It would be great to crush those Serbs and Montenegrins. But what for such cheaply acquired laurels if we have to pay for them with a European crisis and if then we have to fight on two or maybe three fronts and not be able to respond?
Berthold	Your Majesty, mind that the Germans do not hear what you are saying. Kaiser would not be happy. We shall arrange it all to look as if the Serbs planned a sudden attack on us.
Franz Joseph	As a rule, a sudden attack happens against the attacker and less often against the one being attacked. A sudden attack is a surprise, a necessary defensive act which can cause fright among those who are attacking you.
Berthold	You do like a joke, your Majesty.
F Ferdinand	My great grandfather was right when he said: our peoples are all foreigners to one another. They do not understand each other. They hate each other. They do not succumb to the same illness at the same time. They need to be mixed with each other. Of their antipathy order is born and general peace of their hatred. We must see to it that it remains so. I am for war too but a limited one. Some day, not right now.

Berthold	After its defeat by Japan, Russia embarked on reforms and reconstruction of the army and the entire state. It will not be ready for several years to come. The best option, nota bene, is a preventive war with Serbia. Russia will not interfere and we shall rout Serbia. In this way we shall exclude Russia from the Balkans as its zone of interest. We shall prevent its access to warm seas.
Franz Joseph	Don't forget that Karadjordjeviches are not russophiles whatever people say about them. Alexander was an obedient tool in the hands of our consul Radosavljevich and even Peter, after the May coup, was much friendlier toward us. He owed us, in part, his ascent to the throne. From Belgrade Peter casts sceptical looks at Russia because of its selfish politics. So, there is room there for different solutions.
Berthold	Politics is always selfish. In 1848 we were saved from the insurgence in Hungary by the Russian intervention. And then mankind stood in awe of Austria's treachery because it supported the enemies of Russia in the Crimean War. Life is short and is made of many betrayals. So forget Karadjordjeviches. Do not ever, please, tread on the toes of the militaristic circles. The only thing that is certain, nota bene, is our alliance with Germany. German education, German poets, German philosophy, after all/
Franz Joseph	/is not the fabric but the adornment of one's own home with which the people of judges and executioners decorate their emptiness. Now, in a new war, German poetry will receive new impetus. Of all the peoples whose mind has been befogged by their image of themselves as the chosen people, the Germans are most often identified by the way in which they constantly remind themselves that they are Germans. The Jews have, verbally at least, obeyed their commandment! Thou shalt not kill!"
Berthold	That is what you say about the people of poets and thinkers?
Franz Joseph	They can be so crude, can't they? To promote without restraint Kant's categorical imperative as the philosophical excuse for "always strike hard", come on, please! Kant himself would caution them because of all

	that savagery.
Berthold	But, Your Majesty, you are German!
Franz Joseph	The Habsburgs are Swiss, it's not the same. There is a difference, Count Berthold.
F Ferdinand	*[Takes a sip of wine]* I think the Hungarians are worse. You know that I publicly declare that I hate Hungary. But this Tokaji wine is quite okay. *[He goes to the window and watches the snow as it gently falls]*
F Ferdinand	Last Saturday I killed fifty nine wild hogs. One escaped. The alpine peaks glowed red magnificently as the sun was setting. The view was breathtaking. By the end of the next year I shall kill my three thousandth deer. It seems it's snowing. This conversation is over, isn't it? *[F Ferdinand bows and exits]*
Franz Joseph	He's an idiot. Cannot hide the impatience of a crown prince. He never applauds in the theatre. He lacks precisely what is extremely important in Austria: personal consideration, charm and nice manners. Those disagreeable, cold and fixed eyes! He has no sense of music, no sense of humour and his wife is the same; that is what their morganatic marriage looks like! Cruel, arrogant and often insane; he will cause some disaster, mark my words. He speaks about the Hungarians like this before you only because your wife is Hungarian. *[Franz Joseph takes a sip]*
Franz Joseph	But he is right about one thing: this Tokaji is really good. Oh! First class! *[Blackout]*

Belgrade 1

Jack
: Vojislav Tankosich, Major of the Serbian Army, Chetnik commander, one of the founders of the Black Hand clandestine military group.

Graeme
: Dragutin Dimitrijevich Apis, Lieutenant Colonel of the Serbian Army, leading member of Black Hand military group, head of the Intelligence Bureau in the Ministry of War.

Gareth
: Alexander Karadjordjevich, Crown Prince of the Kingdom of Serbia, Commander of the First Army.

Gerard
: A secret place at dusk, some time before Easter 1913. Heavy rain pours down the windows.

Apis
: Most grateful for the audience, Your Royal Highness.

Alexander
: Never mind that, Lieutenant Colonel Dimitrijevich! God has forgotten us.

Tankosich	*[With his mouth full]* God has not forgotten us. He simply does not care.
Alexander	I see you do not observe Lent, gentlemen!
Tankosich	A man who fasts is called a sinner. Your Royal Highness still has stomach trouble since the typhoid? Or are you really fasting?
Alexander	Both.
Apis	Why all these bodyguards who came with Your Royal Highness? Doesn't mutual support mean mutual trust as well?
Alexander	With all due respect, gentlemen, the two of you have already liquidated a Serbian dynasty. Just a little bit of caution, do not take it to heart too much. Look at the situation around us. Everything is changing.
Apis	Nothing is changing. Only friends change.
Alexander	The Balkan War can take some time. And even if it is short, it will turn, I'm afraid, into something much bigger.
Tankosich	Well, all right then. Let's win this one first. We shall deal with the later one afterwards.
Apis	And that afterwards means the liberation of all South Slavs, and especially the Serbs to make myself clearer, from the Austro-Hungarian shackles. If the big shots meddle, three, maybe four empires will cave in or my name isn't Apis! We failed to liquidate Franz Joseph two years ago which doesn't mean we won't do it one of these days.
Tankosich	Him and a couple more.
Alexander	You started even the Balkan War at your own initiative, Major Tankosich! You turned a skirmish with Arnauts at Merdare into a battle without the authorisation by the competent command. You attacked a Turkish observation post at your own initiative! Hell breaks loose wherever you turn up!
Tankosich	But I was still awarded the star with swords and was promoted to Major. I was never short of a minimum of personal initiative, thank God.
Alexander	Mind you two that the Government, also endowed with a minimum of personal initiative, does not send you to early retirement. Personal courage would not be of much help then.
Apis	Right. Wouldn't Your Royal Highness also have a say in

	that?
	[Alexander goes to the window. Watches the rain]
Alexander	Maybe, some. As the head of the Intelligence Bureau of the Ministry of War you are very well informed and you surely know that every influence spreads only so far.
Apis	I do. That is why I also know that last year Lieutenant Colonel Zhivkovich founded an informal officer organisation called the White Hand. Don't you think it stands out like a sore thumb for the officers of the Black Hand? Or do you think that such a name is pure coincidence?
Alexander	I'd rather not talk about it.
Apis	Fine, let it torment you within.
Alexander	And even if I told you, you would not believe me.
Apis	Then don't tell me. There are already enough things I don't believe in.
Alexander	It seems it's raining. I must leave you, gentlemen. Face the facts.
Tankosich	You have not eaten anything, Crown Prince.
	[Blackout]

Berlin 2

Gareth — Stadtschloss in Berlin, 1914, on the eve of the assassination in Sarajevo. Sun scatters around its liquid gold.

Wilhelm — As we already knew, Russia is not ready for war. The Russia of Nicholas II is a remarkably poorly organised and corrupt state. It believes its myth about its own invincibility although it has suffered numerous defeats. The Russian "steam-roller", a poorly equipped army of a million and a half troops and three million reservists, exists on paper only. So, they will not dare engage in a war. Even if our soldiers set against them, they will be back before the leaves fall. Long live the steadfast loyalty of the Nibelungs! We shall draw deep from the well of German fairy-tales. This is the old road, our mysticism and our German baroque, Klopstock and Herder, Goethe and Schiller, Kant and Fichte, Beethoven, Wagner! Vivat!
[Toasting]

Moltke — Vivat! Your Majesty is a world wonder of strategic farsightedness!

Tirpitz — The fact is that the Russians are not ready. And won't be until 1916. On the other side is the Risk Fleet Theory: that our fleet, which is no longer half as powerful as the English one, will dissuade the British from attempting the naval blockade in the North Sea - will still be what it has been: a risk theory. If the British do that, the role of our navy will be a sad one. "A town built on a hill cannot be hidden".

Moltke — May the Lord punish England! I never doubted that the British would take part in the conflict. British selfish politics has not changed, von Tirpitz. They have been preparing for the war for a long time. Though, we have not sat idle either. After all, war is inevitable; everybody is tied up by the clauses. And it will be worse than anyone could imagine. And it won't be short. I also understand the concern regarding the effects it will produce.

Wilhelm — Von Moltke, you underestimate the moral forces driving the war! Such gloomy thoughts are out of place on

such a glorious day. It is high time for the spirit to soar! There is no room for anxiety or sickly worries! It is time to be serious and proudly dignified! The glow of ancient greatness illuminates our era! The people fully support us. Bismarck was right: "Our people are pure joy!" A people are a spring in which you can refresh your soul! And anyway, people have nothing else to do. I measure everything by the fear and disgrace suffered. I have my measuring yard. That is how I know what to charge. After this June there will be no going back. Fear has risen like a light wind over the sea. The epoch is at the breaking point once again. No more dirges! There are no more criteria for the reality. The war can begin. And even if there are crimes, they will be holy crimes! Germany will no longer suffer from the complex of a younger child. Everything will unfold as in a well-rehearsed theatre piece. And don't you start goggling when a general loses some eighty thousand soldiers! Battles are not battles unless they are rich in loss! I promise you victory even in this world. I promise you that the soul who respects this plan shall not lose. Where others fall, we shall rise! Where others hate, we shall love! Where all die, we shall live! A German has no other aspiration but to stay in his country and make an honest living out of his colonies. We must hammer this into the heads of the whole world once and for all. Reign over palaces and broad borders is what lies ahead of us. The main thing is for our men to fight well, the rest will come of its own. And the British envy, the French vengefulness and the Russian rapacity – there's the answer as to who is responsible for the war. But, the hand of God is creating a new world and working miracles.
[They drink up the champagne]

Wilhelm   We must not allow old Franz Joseph to waver at the last moment and slide into the world of intimate absurdities. Let him seize the events that are at our door to realise his old intention to subjugate the big-headed Slavs. Serb nationalism and expansionism are playing into his hands. With the Serbs, the axe is a piece of furniture. They were far too successful in the Balkan Wars. Vienna must make the best of its golden

	opportunity. Of course, they will get our unconditional support straightaway. They were handed a blank cheque a long time ago! The ability of the southerners to enthuse must be directed and regulated by the German seriousness. Ultimatums will be flying about like chaff this summer! And the British might still give up and keep out of the conflict. Who knows? I read in today's press that there were no bathrooms in Downing Street. So, what do you say to that? It's just like them!
Moltke	Right, but that does not mean that they have not had a bath in a hundred years.
Wilhelm	How? You look like a sceptic to me! The English ruling class is made of Freemasons thoroughly infected by Judas.
Moltke	Most grateful for the audience, Your Majesty. At your service, Your Majesty! [Blackout]

Vienna 2

Jack	Hofburg, Vienna, 1914, on the eve of the assassination in Sarajevo. Sun scatters around its liquid gold.
Berthold	Well, Prince, I wish you a happy and pleasant trip to Sarajevo! Pity you won't have time to hunt in the Bosnian forests. They say that the game there is out of

	this world!
F Ferdinand	Really? Is that so? Could be, could be. Governor Potiorek does not grant General Army Inspector any leisure time. Military manoeuvres, a speech here and there and that's it! I hope nobody will throw a bomb at me! This champagne is quite all right! Vivat! *[They toast]*
Berthold	It is not Hungarian, maybe that's why… French, Brut classic method!
F Ferdinand	This conversation is over, isn't it? *[F Ferdinand bows and leaves]*
Franz Joseph	I am afraid, Count Berthold.
Berthold	There is no courage without fear. The future deceased favourite! As of this historic moment we shall not meet him again.
Franz Joseph	May God have mercy on his soul, may the devil take him away!
Berthold	One of your eyes will be moist, the other one serene. Not more than six gendarmes for Sarajevo, reporting humbly. We need others for Belgrade.
Franz Joseph	But he has more of them as he walks around Vienna!
Berthold	Nota bene, for the world he will forever be a man who was in God's hands; there was no way to prevent it. Many will wonder how the most powerful man in the monarchy could not procure better protection for the journey but a potentate who is no more, has no clout. A potentate can do everything except avoid being killed. But when it does happen, punishment must follow – it is a matter of prestige! It will be a first-rate funeral! And it will be an ultimatum as no other in the modern times. There must be satisfaction, every child will see that. We shall be for peace, of course, but not peace at any cost. We shall lie our heads off. Whether we shall also fight like that is another matter. Anonymity is half the charity; it is the job of diplomacy. But – hush! I leave the rest to the troops! The passions will flare up for a little while, at long last! One has to prepare everything for the Postal Savings Bank to decide to financially support the war. And remember to ask the court photographer to make a nice picture of His Majesty engrossed in the study of the geographic map of the Balkans. But discreetly! Always discreetly!

Leisurely and valiantly! Yes, that would be great! It wouldn't hurt either to have a clever journalist - as of now. A comprehensible link between language and war has to be established. A practical fairy-tale, a poetic means. Then we can rely on their spiritual ecstasy. Ideals bring purification to the people. It would not be nice to have a small generation caught unawares by this great time. In this great time any small-mindedness is out of the question. Nota bene, one may not succumb to the poison of pacifism. Wars are a blessing for ideals! Times of peace are dangerous times. Wars are the processes of purification and cleansing, they are the sown fields of virtue and the way to awaken heroes. The honour of the fatherland must mean everything! Our conscience is clear! This is the true Austrian realissimum! This will be a war that our fatherland was drawn into. A defensive war! Although, this sounds as if we shall have to apologise. But, all will wear a cross on their chest!

Franz Joseph I wear it on my back! No serious individual will think that the relatively militarily weak Austro-Hungary is acting alone. And Kaiser is bringing pressure to bear as if it were the end of the world! Egging on and on. Serbia must die whether it likes it or not! Blah-blah-blah! Never mind that the Young Bosnians are not Greater Serbs but idealists who declare themselves as Yugoslavs or Serbocroats, inspired by pan-Slavic and leftist ideas. Great disaster is looming ahead. I'm afraid that those who clamour today will weep tomorrow. Perhaps there is still time left for strategic retreat. Strategic retreat is always a success.

Berthold You are almost a peace monger, Your Majesty! With all due respect, the honour of the fatherland must mean everything! Prince Eugene's march resounds once more! What an imperial vista! Everyone needs a bit of a fight and storm. We shall give Serbia short shrift. It will finally pay for all its plots against the Monarchy. All the rest will come automatically. A sea of light will shine! But what do you say about our diplomacy? That job requires courage! One hit after the other! We did not start the war, we only wished for it! If only the ultimatum is not prevented! We shall be, so to say,

	compelled to let them attack us. Young Bosnia, Young Turkey, Young Italy, Young Poland, they all have one goal in mind: destruction of multinational monarchies! So why should we feel embarrassed then? Oh! What a lovely war! Our deeds pave the way for us and our goal is the starting point of glory! Austria will resurrect as a phalanx from the universal fire! The myth about Austria shall live!
Franz Joseph	Myths are public dreams, dreams are private myths. And now everybody can hardly wait to gird the sabre! Habsburgs hover above the world peace like Damocles' sword! I am afraid. Antichrist is near. Last night I dreamed about the capitulation on land, at sea and in air! And I dreamed that General Geza von Lakati Nemesfalva et Kutyavilag Faluszeg ingloriously retreated from Galicia; that he shouted hooray at a wrong place again and then came to me to explain that he had simply drawn back from the enemy and is only hauling him along! They have talked me into a world war! I have considered it all carefully but there, there's nothing else I can do! Without any rhyme or reason I turn millions of people into corpses and cripples. Oh, Lord, do not make me a witness! Do not let it happen, for the love of blessed blood of Jesus! The eternity is already eroding! We have burnt out! Who is responsible, my dear homeland?
Berthold	Most grateful for the audience, Your Majesty! At your service, Your Majesty! *[Blackout]*

Belgrade 2

Gerard   Belgrade, the confluence of the Sava and the Danube, 1914, on the eve of the assassination in Sarajevo. Sun scatters its liquid gold.

Tankosich   The black and yellow banner, there it is! Let the Austrians watch us across the river as we raise toasts! They have powerful gadgets! Pardon my French, Your Royal Highness, they can see pretty clearly how I scratch my arse!

Alexander   Enough of these indecent pranks, for heavens' sake! Enough of them! There is nothing to toast to. If yet another stupid thing happens, my government will have to make no end of allowances to Austro-Hungary. *[Tankosich offers champagne to Alexander and Apis. Alexander refuses]*

Alexander   Thank you. Would you like some tea?
Tankosich   No, not now, not ever!
Apis   Long live Serbia!
[They toast]
Tankosich   Justice shall win!
Alexander   If you ask for justice, you live in the wrong century.

Tankosich	I am not asking for anything except that their government and diplomats wade in a sea of blood and tears, may their brood be cursed! See that observation post there? The first thing I will do on the first night of fire, will be to go there with my Chetniks, disarm and undress the guards, send them to Zemun bare-arsed and hoist the Serbian flag! And then return across the river to Belgrade wearing Austrian uniform, go to the Gold Sturgeon and order a round of drinks for all! And then I'll find and beat the cabinet ministers who will try to flee from the city the very first night and sow panic among the people. *[Shows his fist to Austria-Hungary across the river]*
Tankosich	Haughty hyenas, I'll make a stew on your fire! I'll drink your blood! As for those Serbs in Bosnia whom I catch in Austrian uniforms, I'll cut off their ears personally, curse their Turkish cross!
Apis	Your Highness, please pay no attention to Tankosich's manners. A lyrical beast, so to speak! Slightly off his rocker, but very likeable! In spite of the devil and death and the screams of our enemies.
Alexander	You are no better, Lieutenant Colonel Dimitrijevich! You have made a huge step in the wrong direction; it's so like the Serbs! We've never learned anything from fate. Do you really think that the spreading of your net around Bosnia was invisible to the Austrians? As if they do not know what you yelled about in the Gold Sturgeon! Major Tankosich's conduct is beyond the pale! How he, for instance, fires at apples on the shoulders of his soldiers! The Black Hand did not help the state politics at all in this case. I told you ages ago that the Russians had asked me to tell you not to start anything now. You refused to listen. And now this horrible situation threatens us! You should know that Mr Pashich, our Prime Minister, has notified the Viennese Court that the assassination was being prepared. Austro-Hungary was authorised, at the Berlin Congress, to occupy Bosnia for thirty years! And even before that, Russia undertook not to mind Austria's annexation of Bosnia after the expiration of that period. That is how it is – whether you like it or not! The Black Hand's control of Young Bosnia, your "Unification or death" could

	have waited a little with its cheap patriotic phraseology! Who will believe that the official Serbia had no hand in this? Serbia committed all sorts of violence in the Balkan Wars, nobody knows it better than you. You think it's been forgotten? A people is finished when it hauls dead phrases to places where it brings their content back to life. This is a proof that that people's life has come to its end.
Apis	You are aware that I sent one of my officers to Bosnia to stop this thing? He was refused, Your Royal Highness. And, at the same time, Austro-Hungary did not take Pashich's warning seriously. It did not want to. What does it tell you, your Royal Highness?
Alexander	That there will be a war. That there will be a horrible war. You know nothing about world history.
Tankosich	World history appears here twice a day, your Royal Highness. In other words, much too often to enjoy the necessary authority. However – many enemies, much honour! Death is not foreign to us! I shall have to produce wonders of heroism again. The house I live in is right across the street from the German Mission. I shall set fire to them first. And my last cry in the next war shall be: You who want to die, follow me!
Alexander	I am speechless. Some help that would be! Just like the fact that once, in a tavern, you slapped in the face a young British correspondent called Winston Churchill because you did not like his coverage of Serbia. And then he was seen off to the Belgrade railway station under police escort. And an official apology had to be written. Well, now he is the First Lord of the Admiralty! And who knows what else he will be?
Tankosich	He can be whatever he likes, I don't give a hoot! And, after all, neither does he.
Apis	Most grateful for the audience, Your Royal Highness! *[Blackout]*

Sarajevo

[Two shots]

Anywhere in Europe

Colporteur Crown Prince and wife killed! Special issue! Conspirators arrested! Special issue! Everybody shattered with grief! Discontent in England! Despair in Russia! Depression in Italy! Utter confusion in Belgium! Demoralisation in Serbia! Defeatism in Montenegro! Anger in Austria! Threats in Germany! Special issue! Special issue! Austro-Hungary declares war on Serbia! Germany declares war on Russia! Germany declares war on France! Germany declares war on Belgium! Great Britain declares war on Germany! Montenegro declares war on Austro-Hungary! Austro-Hungary declares war on Russia! Serbia declares war on Germany! Montenegro declares war on Germany! France declares war on Austro-Hungary! Britain declares war on Austro-Hungary! Special issue! Russia has not declared war on anyone! Special issue! Montenegro declares war on everyone! Special issue! Nobody has declared war on Great Britain! Great Britain declares war on everyone! Special issue!

[Dominos topple]

London 2

Grump — CNN is worried because Ukraine is coughing. Don't count me in the group of the concerned, please. That TV station is chronically concerned with the fate of the entire world. From one hour to the other they flood me with information about the concern that Ukraine could be split up. Why was the secession of Ukraine, all with Soviet nuclear warheads, a merry and relaxing event once and now this situation provokes the formula of concern? Isn't that the logic of unfinished thought?

Optimist — A humanitarian intervention is what is needed there!

Grump — It would be nice to help the population of Crimea but the problem is that they don't ask for help! The situation there does not require a humanitarian intervention, the humanitarian intervention requires a situation and there is no situation! And without that slogan about the humanitarian intervention, war becomes a direct naturalistic war for interests, for resources, control and power. There was applause when the Soviet Union fell apart, when Czechoslovakia fell apart, when Yugoslavia fell apart. What criteria determine that it is a bad thing when some borders fall and that when other borders fall it is a good thing? When the West bombs Serbia – Merciful Angel, when the Russians take Crimea - Merciless Angel! How did the Western political thought find itself in such a schizophrenic situation with political loss of face? Putin is not as likeable as the Uruguayan president, but he put the key question to the democratic world.

Optimist — And that is?

Grump — He asked them why they support the protests in Kiev but not those in Sarajevo.

Optimist — And they?

Grump — And they did not know the answer. Then he asked them another question.

Optimist — Which was?

Grump — How is it that they support the revolutionary government in Kiev but not the revolutionary government on Crimea? Or, in plain English: how is it that the referendum in the Falklands is acceptable but the referendum in Crimea is not?

Optimist	And they did not know the answer again?
Grump	How did you guess! But, one should not trust the West when it talks about democracy just as one should not trust Russia when it talks about ideals.
Optimist	Spare me your modern grumping! The ceremony was beautiful! One hundred years! Everybody remembers fallen heroes. Paying respects to them! It's so nice! And so exciting! And how dignified! No luxury, just quiet grief!
Grump	Yes. Stars and coryphaei swarming around. Your Optimistic presence goes without saying. A dark morning. Prayers at the army cemetery always go down well. The situation of the fallen heroes was truly remarkable. They atoned for unknown guilt. Poison, night and fatherland. Advance, advance! Courage! On to the Somme! The victory is ours! Advance! Go! Go! You will all die so behave accordingly! God is with you, fire assiduously at the enemy! You held the positions, my beautiful ones. The enemy in front, the fatherland behind. Who is worse? And eternal stars above. They should have distributed lachryimaria to the politicians on this occasion, to preserve the tears shed today for the victims of yesterday for another war. They are all artists of lies, they do not believe them themselves, but want to hear them because a lie tells them what they feel more clearly. A genre image is all that is left: lithe and brilliant youth bursting with awesome energy burns with zeal and a feeling of importance, a feeling of affiliation with the heavenly people, a new and strong race, brimming with will. Eyes turned to stone under the helmet, eyes that spread terror, future builders on the destroyed foundations of the world. To each his own. To a hero a grave. He wanted to free the world and the world got free of him. And then, out of the blue, peace, silence, quiet. Smoke spirals up above the battle-field, shadows sway among the trees, a bloody sun sets. A bottle of real champagne and a tin of real caviar arrive at the headquarters. Fresh rolls and flowers of all colours, radishes and damask tablecloth. Such contrasts exist only on the frontline.
Optimist	Aren't you exaggerating? Every epoch has its war.
Grump	Every epoch has its plague. Every epoch has the

epidemic it deserves. And this one was such that perhaps for the first time since the creation of the world, the devil cried: "Oh, hell!" And all that because of a handful of unimaginative mediocrities! One hundred years! And academics are still arguing as to who was the editor in chief, who was Mars and who was Mercury of the world war? Some blame Germany which had the power to prevent the catastrophe by withdrawing its support of Austria's attack on Serbia. Some say that Russia did not want war either, at least not right then. Nor did Serbia, exhausted by the Balkan Wars. Others claim that Serbia was to blame because its nationalism and expansionism were the strongest disruptive forces as is seen best in the official Belgrade's support of the Black Hand. Still others say that the culprits behind the world conflict were the Austro-Hungarian, German and Russian army hawks. Some claim that diplomacy failed. Today, German authors accuse Britain, among others. An academic work asserting that Princip was a Jew and a free mason stands out. Gabriel, not Gavrilo! Original, isn't it? Its author is truly possessed of imagination, and soul, and wit and opinion! Mazel tov! However, it seems that the only result was millions of tonnes of sunk spirit. The thunder then ceased to roar and we do not know what it wanted from us. There were two hundred and fifty thousand minors in the British armed forces. Sidney Lewis was only 12 when, drunk on patriotism, he was deployed with a mortar unit on the Somme. I only hope that it is true that on the Day of Judgment no fiddling will be tolerated. And that it will not be possible then to manipulate things in one's favour as we are accustomed to. And I want to tell you that it is more pleasing to God to pay tribute to the majesty of death at the tombs of boys and men, mothers and children who died of bullets or starvation than at the tombs in which rest those who thought about it carefully and then caused it with one stroke of a pen.

Optimist I am aghast! One's heart breaks hearing you speak.
Grump What you will. War turns life into a nursery where the other one invariably started it first and where one boasts about the same crime he reproaches the other

	for. Incredible sentences the madness of which resounds lastingly were truly uttered, the most incredible acts really happened. And I tell you: the scum simply wreaked havoc! You are an Optimist and you simply do not want to see people who eat shit.
Optimist	Repairer of the world! – Big deal! You have always been a pessimist in matters of war! Well, stay in your corner and grump! What a faint heart! Every war ends in peace. Don't you see that because of that a great epoch has set in?
Grump	I knew it when it was small and it will become small again. What gigantic tininess! The world war was the result of a relatively minor international crisis, wrong estimates, fear that prestige would be lost and stubborn commitment to a very complex system of military delusions and political alliances. It was a war of illusions. The ultimatum to Serbia was such that it was clear in advance that it would not accept it. And even if it had, no form of acceptance, however pitiful, would satisfy the aggressor. Only because some thought that the timing was perfect! And then somebody called it well-advised politics. They should have denied their bodies and their souls to the fatherland. They should have all done precisely that.
Optimist	What does individual suffering mean? Just as little as individual life! And isn't suffering God's thing? Man's eyes are directed upwards. Man needs more than bread to live!
Grump	So he needs to wage wars so as not to have it.
Optimist	What will you, that's how it is in a war! All you care for is grumping! I am and will be an Optimist! Through damage peoples become –
Grump	- stupid.
Optimist	Wouldn't it be nice if the fatherland thought like you do!
Grump	That is how the fatherland thinks.
Optimist	In the end morning light always conquers darkness! And life recovers from painful deeds!
Grump	From painful deeds of a greedy civilisation.
Optimist	There, you're grumping again! Greed is good. It has marked the evolution of the humankind. It created civilisation! It is good in all its forms!

Grump	Right word at the right time! The word of an Optimist! We finally agree about something. Yes! And that's how we got a greedy civilisation, in which greed produces wars, in which greed proclaims peace, in which greed determines the price of a staple on that folder you keep on your desk. And in which greedy heads of greedy states cannot be called to account for their greedy actions. But we have always compensated for our tyrants by our own ranks. And then the end comes and there is nothing left. Kyrie eleison!
Optimist	Democracy has won, excuse me!
Grump	You really do come out with it! In the societies belonging to the democratic world one per cent of the population owns fifty per cent of the total wealth. Don't tell me that you truly believe that democratic story!
Optimist	You hold nothing sacred! What idea do you advocate?
Grump	As a grump, I am bound to see everything black. Ergo, I advocate the idea that God did not create man as a consumer or a producer but as a man. That daily bread is not the objective of life. That life is not based on exclusivity and interests of business. That man has been placed in time in order to have time rather than to arrive somewhere faster with his legs than with his heart. What will become of you, Europe? You have not recovered from your most dangerous truths. Is it burning all over again? The epoch is at a breaking point again? What a dirge! We thought our history, however farcical, will be repeated in a nicer form, not looking like tragedy, at least on the outside. Germany wanted to be an imperial power and today it is, even without the army. And yet it is too small to dominate the continent and too strong to play it alone; it is again a semi-hegemonist. Austro-Hungary is gone and it was a good state. It has turned out, however, that its ultimatum was really stupid. Serbia's border is, surprise, surprise, at Merdare again, at a place where Commander Tankosich started the first Balkan War without the authorisation by the competent command. Yugoslavia, for which the Young Bosnians fought and which was also a good state, is gone too. And Bosnia has again an Austrian governor in Sarajevo, just like one hundred years ago. And now, one hundred years

	later, there are demonstrations across Bosnia again. The Archival Library has burnt down and with it the evidence of crimes. And Bosnia is still the mirror of Europe! Like Ukraine! For the first time since the fall of the Berlin Wall capitalism feels fear which it needs so much to rein in its insatiable appetite. Long live the balance of fear! Without it, that immense capitalist mouth devours even what it cannot digest. We make up for the absence of ideology with the ideology of borders. Here we are, we are returning to the borders defined at the Berlin Congress, which means that the world wars of the twentieth century, not only the first one, the second one too, were waged without any rhyme or reason! Where were we, Europe? Nowhere! What did we do, Europe? Nothing! All those dead and mutilated and – oh, well, what can you do? War was a child's game compared to the peace that was established; a delta leading to the big water of insanity. After the war, more wars and more suffering. Are you happy? I leave it to your practiced optimism to choose.
Optimist	'Happy' is a non-word! Call it love for one's fatherland, you idealists; hatred of the enemy, you nationalists; call it a sport, you modern men; an adventure, you romantics; call it the delight of strength, you connoisseurs of the soul; the last days, you grumps - I call it the liberated mankind!
Grump	You call it – what?
Optimist	The liberated mankind! *[Blackout]*

...

FINGER TRIGGER BULLET GUN

A.D. 2014

Karlu Krausu

Prolog - London 1

DRAMATIS PERSONAE
- Edward VII, Kralj Ujedinjenog Kraljevstva, britanskih Dominiona i Imperator Indije, mrtav

- Optimista 1, uskoro mrtav

- Zanovetalo 1, uskoro mrtav takodje

Ulice Londona. Sahrana Edwarda VII, 20. maj 1910. Promiče kovčeg.

Optimista   Jadni naš kralj! Još od kada je iznenada izgubio je svest u Berlinu prošle godine, strepeo sam svakoga dana nad njegovim zdravljem. Ah, tempi passati, vi i sami znate, nemo propheta in sua patria i svi putevi vode u Rim!
Zanovetalo   Bronhitis. Dvadeset cigareta dnevno minimum. S tim se nije šaliti.
Optimista   Jadni naš kralj! Kažu da je umro posle nekoliko uzastopnih srčanih udara. Napatio se, jadni naš kralj. Kada mu je Princ od Velsa saopštio da je njegov konj Witch of the Air pobedio na Kempton Parku tog popodneva, samo je rekao: "Yes, I have heard of it. I am very glad". Bile su to njegove poslednje reči. Umro

	je petnaest minuta kasnije. Može li srce koje oseća da ne učestvuje? Pogledajte: devet krunisanih glava u povorci, petoro prestolonaslednika, sedam kraljica...
Zanovetalo	Da! Mislite li da će ova divna uverira ostati bez nastavka?
Optimista	Kako molim? Zar i sada još možete da negirate? Pravo ste zanovetalo! Pronose se glasine da se šire glasine! Eto, to je!
Zanovetalo	Cena krvi je pala, cena mesa je skočila.
Optimista	Ali, svi oni su jedna velika familija, nećaci i ujaci jedan drugom! Oni su so zemlje i svetlo sveta! Pokojnik je bio brat majke nemačkog Kajzera, koji je ovde, vidite li ga? Eno ga, i to u uniformi britanskog feldmaršala! Braća udovice su kraljevi Danske i Grčke, u srodstvu je i ruski dvor, kao i balkanske kraljevske kuće...
Zanovetalo	Što ih neće sprečiti da se već sutradan medjusobno pokolju! Tu ima priča iza priča. Ne želite da vidite da, kroz tretman Kajzera, Nemačka po ceo bogovetni dan samo proverava svoju želju da bude poštovana i uvažavana.
Optimista	Ali, bar postoje neki ideali! I nekakva solidarnost, pa makar i u smrti! Zar to ne znači da zlo prolazi?
Zanovetalo	Zlo najbolje napreduje iza ideala. I iza ideje lažne solidarnosti.
Optimista	Ali, ideja daje mogućnost ozdravljenja!
Zanovetalo	Za ideju se može umreti, a da se ipak ne ozdravi. Jer, ne umire se za ideju, već na njoj. Za nju se čak umire, a da je uopšte i nema. Od nje se umire, a da se to i ne zna.
Optimista	To je igra reči! A vi ste jedno zanovetalo!
Zanovetalo	Jesam, mada priznajem da ste vi optimista.
Optimista	Ali pogledajte! Kakva idilična slika!
Zanovetalo	Verovatno i poslednja slika evropske idile.
Optimista	Prekinite, zaboga, barem u ovom času! Pogledajte ovaj bal sloge! Uncle of Europe je umro, a evo ih: King George V, Frederick VII od Danske, Haakon VII od

	Norveške, Alfonso XIII od Španije, Manuel II od Portugalije, Albert I od Belgije, Ferdinand I od Bugarske, Wilhelm II od Nemačke i Prusije, prinčevi prestolonaslednici, evo nadvojvode Franza Ferdinanda od Austrije, evo Aleksandra od Srbije, evo Marije Fjodorovne, supruge pokojnog imperatora od cele Rusije, stigao je i rodjak imperatora Japana, bivši američki predsednik Theodor Roosevelt, kineski princ... So zemlje i svetlo sveta!
Zanovetalo	Ali, ako so obljutavi, čime će se ona osoliti?
Optimista	Pssst! Pogledajte ono devojče, zgodna zar ne?
Zanovetalo	Prestanite, to je prostitutka!
	[Pada mrak]

- - - - -

Zanovetalo	Evo me, stojim na Božjem dlanu. Britanska IV armija na Sommi, Battle of Fromelles, 19. juli 1916. Ne znam zašto sam uopšte promolio glavu iznad polusrušenog zida tog jutra. Ništa nisam čuo, ali to ništa došlo je s leve strane. Nije me bolelo. Sivi oblaci su bili iznad, Optimisto. Zatim sam valjda umro.
Optimista	Evo me, stojim na Božjem dlanu. Poginuo sam pet dana pre tebe, zanovetalo. British Expeditionary Force, BEF. Bazentin Ridge. To jutro sam neprekidno povraćao. Toliko prosutih utroba! A onda se desilo. Jednostavno se desilo. Ma, nije ni važno.
Zanovetalo	Oluja je stigla. Noć je bila divlja. Uništena je Božija slika i prilika.
Optimista	Na kraju od smrti nastaje ples. Od mržnje nastaje šala. Od bede nastaje prevara. Šta li je onda to?
Zanovetalo	Šta li je onda to?

Berlin 1

DRAMATIS PERSONAE
- Kaiser Wilhelm II, Poslednji nemački imperator i pruski kralj

- Helmuth Johann Ludwig von Moltke, Šef Nemačkog Generalnog štaba

- Alfred von Tirpitz, Veliki admiral, Državni sekretar Nemačke mornarice

Statdschloss in Berlin. Neformalni susret Nemačkog kraljevskog ratnog saveta od 8. decembra 1912. Prisutni su nagnuti nad mapama koje su na stolu. Dime se cigare. Snažan vetar povija grane ispod velikih prozora.

Moltke   Najusrdnije hvala na audijenciji, ekselencijo! Sluga ponizni, ekselencijo! Mi smo spremni! Što pre rat počne, to bolje za nas! Za ono što mi sada želimo da postignemo mora da se bije! Osvajanje postaje zakon neophodnosti. Uspešna država zna da započne rat u za sebe najpovoljnijem momentu. Francuska mora da bude tako kompletno zgažena, da nam se više nikad ne ispreči na putu.

Wilhelm	Nemačka borba za preživljavanje ostavlja Britance potpuno ravnodušnim. Slepi od inferiornih osećanja, pridružuju se Slovenima i Romanima. Već godinama sa Francuzima prave zajedničke planove. Rusija će podržavati Srbiju, što očigledno već i čini. Monarsi Evrope, svih ovih godina moje vladavine, nisu obraćali pažnju na ono što govorim: da je postojeći status quo u Evropi, za nas i naše saveznike - neodrživ! Nisu obraćali pažnju uopšte! Uskoro, sa našom velikom mornaricom koja će stajati iza mojih reči, pokazivaće više uvažavanja. Sledeći rat će se zvati nemački rat! Jer, rat nije slučajna nezgoda! Nemačka više neće popunjavati svoju kolekciju uvreda! Odgovoriće gvozdenom pesnicom i sevanjem mača! Napominjem da će to biti rat koji mi nismo želeli, rat koji nam je bio nametnut.
Moltke	Ruse i Srbe razbićemo u komadiće!
Wilhelm	Ostavite me na miru sa Srbijom, von Moltke, Srbija je sporedno ratište!
Moltke	Mi smo spremni. Prvi korak bi bio rušenje belgijske neutralnosti, što je već odavno jasno. Car Nikolaj II je veoma slab, što je takodje već odavno jasno. Spremni smo, a drugi nisu. Nećemo ćekati da Rusi modernizuju svoju armiju i dovrše pruge koje prave prema našim teritorijama.
Tirpitz	Nismo spremni.
	[Tišina]
Tirpitz	Velika tuča se mora malo odložiti. Neophodno je da napravimo podmorničku bazu na Helgolandu i da proširimo Kilski kanal. Bez toga gubimo rat.
	[Tišina]
Moltke	Koliko je vremena potrebno da se to uradi, admirale?
Tirpitz	Godinu i po.
	[Tišina]
Moltke	Onda, idemo u rat 1914.
Wilhelm	Treba smisliti nekakav alibi, nešto kao povod za rat. Najbolje na Balkanu. Pazite, potrebno je da nam se priredi jedna zaista izuzetna provokacija. Malko sejanje nesloge nije uošte loše, nije na odmet, krajnje je vreme. *[Ode do prozora. Gleda grane na vetru]*
Wilhelm	Mornarica da se sprema za sukob za Rusijom, ali i sa Britanijom, ako postane neophodno. Započeti kampanju u štampi kako Nemačka mora da nastupi na

strani Austro-Ugarske u slučaju intervencije. Zalihe za vojsku da počnu da se prave. Komitet za mobilizaciju da se oformi. Zlatne rezerve, bankovni depoziti i akcije da se vrate u Nemačku. Aktivirati stari oficirski kadar. Svim visoko pozicioniranim vojnicima narediti da svoje privatne račune u inostranstvu vrate u zemlju. Načiniti plan mobilizacije za istočni front. Neutralizirati mekušce koji se zalažu za mir. Pisaću svim našim i švajcarskim ambasadorima da će verovatno doći do rata u nekoliko sledećih godina. A vama dvojci kažem: rat 1914. Od sada za godinu i po. Nemački rat. Borba za mesto pod suncem! Mi Nemci, koji još imamo ideala, vodićemo sveti odbrambeni rat, a rezultat tog rata može biti jedino mir. Takav mir koji će nam doneti proširenje naših granica na istoku i zapadu i u prekomorskim oblastima - gde nemačka svetska politika mora voditi glavnu reč. A onda ću, posle rata, sledeće zime konačno moći da se malo iščupam na rivijeru. Slani vazduh veoma prija mojim plućima. Čini se da duva vetar.

[Kajzer ispruži desnu ruku, Moltke i Tirpitz je ljube]

Moltke V eličanstvo više nije instrument Boga, već je Bog instrument vašeg veličanstva!

Wilhelm Ha! E, to je dobro!

Beč 1

DRAMATIS PERSONAE

- Franz Joseph I, Austrijski imperator i Apostolski kralj Madjarske.

- Franz Ferdinand of Austria, Austrijski nadvojvoda, Austro-Ugarski i kraljevski princ Madjarske .

- Grof Leopold Berthold, Anton Johann Sigismund Josef Korsinus Ferdinand, Ministar spoljnih poslova Austrije i bivši ambasador u Rusiji.

Hofburg, Beč. Zima 1913. Lagani sneg nad gradom.

Berthold   Najusrdnije hvala na audijenciji, Vaše Carsko i Kraljevsko Veličanstvo. Sluga ponizni, ekselencijo! Javljam pokorno da do polovine ove godine moramo kreirati novu državu, Albaniju! Srbija ne sme izaći na more i nikako ne smeju napraviti zajedničku državu

	Južnih Slovena. Previše je već Slovena i u našoj državi, imaju natpolovičnu većinu! Samo nam treba sad još jedna njihova velika susedna država! U nemačkom delu carstva, nota bene, Nemci čine samo trideset i tri procenta stanovništva! Naša politika na Balkanu ne sme postati iluzija posle ovog Balkanskog rata. Rusi moraju biti sprečeni. Skupilo se dovoljno zapaljivih stvari da izazovu, u za to najpovoljnijim uslovima, eksploziju u čijem će bljesku Rusija biti pozvana da proslavi svoje uspravljanje.
F Ferdinand	Srbe ne volim. Ne treba mi ni jedna srpska šljiva. To je zaverenički narod. Ali carstvo mora iznutra da se preuredi. Slovenski element mora dobiti državnost kao i madjarski. Brojke su neumoljive. Trijalizam može biti rešenje.
Berthold	Bečki militarsti će vas pustiti niz vodu, ako tako nešto glasno kažete.
Franz Joseph	Treba zaustaviti Konrada! Načelnik austrijskog vrhovnog štaba mora da prestane sa tom svojom ratničkom groznicom. Bilo bi divno samleti te Srbe i Crnogorce. Ali čemu jeftino stečene lovorike ako treba da ih platimo evropskom krizom, ako potom moramo da se tučemo možda na dva ili tri fronta, a da ne možemo na to da odgovorimo!
Berthold	Ekselencijo, nemojte da Nemci čuju takve vaše reči. Kajzer ne bi bio srećan. Sredićemo sve da bude tako kao da su nas Srbi planirano iznenada napali.
Franz Joseph	Iznenadni napad se po pravilu dešava protiv onog koji te napada, a redje protiv onog koji se napada. Iznenadni napad predstavlja iznenadjenje, akt nužne odbrane, koji donekle isprepadne onog koji te napada.
Berthold	Vaše Carsko i Kraljevsko Veličanstvo baš voli da se šali.
F Ferdinand	Moj pradeda je imao pravo kada je rekao: naši narodi tudjini su jedan za drugog. Oni se ne razumeju. Oni se mrze. Njih ne obuzima ista bolest u isto vreme. Treba ih slati jedne medju druge. Iz njihove antipatije radja se red, iz njihove mržnje opšti mir. Moramo obezbediti da tako i ostane. I ja sam za rat, ali za ograničeni rat. U perspektivi, ne odmah.
Berthold	Rusija je posle poraza u ratu sa Japanom krenula u reforme i obnovu vojske i celokupne države. Neće biti spremna još nekoliko godina. Najbolja varijanta, nota

	bene, je preventivni rat sa Srbijom. Rusija se neće umešati i zgazićemo Srbiju. Na taj način isključujemo Rusiju sa Balkana kao interesne zone. Sprečićemo njen izlazak na topla mora.
Franz Joseph	Ne zaboravite da Karadjordjevići nisu rusofili, ma šta se pričalo o njima. Aleksandar je bio poslušno orudje našeg konzula Radosavljevića, a i Petar je nakon Majskog prevrata imao daleko više naklonosti prema nama. Dugovao nam je, delimično, svoj dolazak na presto. Petar i sa velikom skepsom gleda iz Beograda na Rusiju, zbog njene sebične politike. Dakle, nije da tu nema prostora za različita rešenja.
Berthold	Nema politike koja nije sebična. Nas je 1848. od bune u Madjarskoj spasila ruska intervencija. A onda je Austrija zadivila čovečanstvo svojim verolomstvom tako što je u Krimskom ratu podržavala neprijatelje Rusije. Život je kratak i sastoji se od mnoštva izdaja. Pustite zato Karadjordjeviće. Nemojte se nikako, ni u kom slučaju, molim vas, zamerati militarističkim krugovima. Jedino što je nota bene sigurno, jeste naše savezništvo sa Nemačkom. Nemačko obrazovanje, nemački pesnici, nemačka filozofija, uostalom...
Franz Joseph	... nije sadržaj, već kićenje sopstvenog doma, kojim narod sudija i dželata kiti svoju prazninu. Sada će, u novom ratu, nemačko pesništvo dobiti nove impulse. Medju svim narodima kojima je mozak popila predstava da su izabrani narod, oni se najčešće identifikuju na taj način što neprestano sami sebe podsećaju da su Nemci. Jevreji su se bar verbalno pridržavali svoje zapovesti: "Ne ubij!"
Berthold	Tako se izjašnjavate o narodu pesnika i mislilaca?
Franz Joseph	Imaju grube ispade, zar ne? Kantovski kategorički imperativ bez ustručavanja reklamirati kao filozofsko opravdanje za "uvek samo čvrsto udri", aj'te, molim vas! Sam Kant bi ih opomenuo zbog takvog divljanja!
Berthold	Ali, vi ste Nemac, ekselencijo!
Franz Joseph	Habsburzi su Švajcarci, nije to isto, grofe Berthold.
F Ferdinand	[Otpije gutljaj vina] Meni su Madjari gori. Vi znate da ja i javno govorim da mrzim Madjarsku. Ali, ovaj Tokajac je sasvim u redu. [Ode do prozora. Gleda sneg koji lagano pada]
F Ferdinand	Prošle subote sam ubio pedeset i devet divljih svinja.

	Jedna je utekla. Bio je prvoklasni crveni odsjaj alpskih vrhova na zalasku sunca. Panorama je bila izvanredna. Do kraja sledeće godine ubiću svog tri hiljaditog jelena. Čini se da pada sneg. Ovaj razgovor je završen, zar ne? [Franz Ferdinand se nakloni i izadje]
Franz Joseph	On je idiot. Ne ume da prikrije svoje prestolonasledničko nestrpljenje. U pozorištu nikada ne aplaudira. Nedostaje mu upravo ono što je u Austriji neizmerno važno: lična predusretljivost, šarm i ugodan način ophodjenja. Te neprijatne, hladne i ukočene oči! Nema smisla za muziku, nema smisla za humor, a takva je i ta njegova žena - eto kako to izgleda u njihovom morganatskom braku! Surov, bahat, a često i lud - on će sasvim sigurno prouzrokovati neku nesreću. Tako govori o Madjarima pred vama, samo zato što vam je supruga Madjarica.
Franz Joseph	Otpije.
Franz Joseph	Ali u jednom je u pravu: ovaj Tokajac je zaista dobar. Ah, prvorazredan!

Beograd 1

DRAMATIS PERSONAE
- Alexander Karadjordjević, Princ prestolonaslednik Kraljevine Srbije, Komandant Prve armije

- Dragutin Dimitrijević Apis, Potpukovnik Srpske armije, vodeći član tajne vojne grupe Crna ruka, šef Obaveštajnog odeljenja Ratnog ministarstva

- Vojislav Tankosić, Major Srpske armije, četnički vojvoda, jedan od osnivača tajne vojne grupe Crna ruka

Sastanak u sumrak na skrovitom mestu izmedju dva Balkanskog rata, pred Uskrs 1913. Sliva se teška kiša niz prozore. Tankosić jede i pije. Apis samo jede. Prestonaslednik niti jede, niti pije.

Apis   Najusrdnije hvala na audijenciji, vaše kraljevsko visočanstvo.

Aleksandar	Pustite sad to, potpukovniče Dimitrijević! Bog nas je zaboravio.
Tankosić	[S punim ustima] Bog nas nije zaboravio. Samo ga baš briga.
Aleksandar	Vidim ne postite pred Uskrs, gospodo oficiri.
Tankosić	Čovek koji posti zove se grešnik. Kraljevsko visočanstvo još ima stomačne probleme od tifusa, ili zaista posti?
Aleksandar	I jedno i drugo.
Apis	Čemu ovoliko obezbedjenje, s kojim je došlo Njegovo kraljevsko visočanstvo? Zar uzajamno pomaganje ne radja i uzajamno poverenje?
Aleksandar	Uz pripadajuće poštovanje gospodo, vas dvojca ste već likvidirali jednu srpsku dinastiju. Mala predostrožnost, ne uzimajte previše k srcu. Pogledajte situaciju svuda oko nas. Sve se menja.
Apis	Ništa se ne menja. Menjaju se samo prijatelji.
Aleksandar	Balkanski rat može potrajati. Čak i ako bude kratak, pretvoriće se, bojim se, u nešto mnogo veće.
Tankosić	Pa, dobro. Prvo njega da završimo pobednički. Posle ćemo ono posle.
Apis	A to posle podrazumeva oslobodjenje svih Južnih Slovena, naročito Srba da se jasnije izrazim, od Austro-Ugarskog jarma. Ako se umešaju veliki, srušiće se tri-četiri carstva, ne zvao se ja Apis! Nismo uspeli da likvidiramo Franza Josepha pre dve godine, što ne znači da nećemo.
Tankosić	I njega i još kojekoga.
Aleksandar	Vi ste majore Tankosiću i Balkanski rat započeli samoincijativno! Čarku sa Arnautima kod Merdara ste pretvorili u bitku, bez odobrenja nadležne komande. Napali ste tursku karaulu samoinicijativno! Gde god se pojavite napravite rusvaj!
Tankosić	Svejedno sam dobio zvezdu s mačevima i unapredjen u majora. Minimum lične inicijative, hvala Bogu, nikada mi nije nedostajao.
Aleksandar	Pazite obojca da vas Vlada, kojoj takodje ne nedostaje minimum lične inicijative, ne penzioniše daleko pre vremena. Sopstvena hrabrost tu ne bi bila od neke naročite pomoći.
Apis	Dobro, valjda bi se i Njegovo kraljevsko visočanstvo tu nešto pitalo?
	[Aleksandar ode do prozora. Gleda kišu]

Aleksandar	Možda, donekle. Kao šef obaveštajnog odeljenja Ratnog ministarstva odlično ste obavešteni i sigurno znate da svaki uticaj ime svoje limite.
Apis	Da. Zato znam i da je potpukovnik Živković prošle godine osnovao neslužbenu oficirsku organizaciju pod nazivom Bela ruka. Da li mislite kako to malo bode oči oficirima koji su u Crnoj ruci. Ili mislite da je davanje takvog imena čista slučajnost?
Aleksandar	Ne bih da govorim o tome.
Apis	Lepo, neka vas muči iznutra.
Aleksandar	I kada bih vam rekao, ne biste verovali.
Apis	Onda mi nemojte reći. Već ne verujem u dovoljno stvari.
Aleksandar	Čini se da pada kiša. Moram da vas napustim, gospodo. Pamet u glavu.
Tankosić	Ništa niste pojeli, prestonaslediče.

Berlin 2

DRAMATIS PERSONAE
- Kaiser Wilhelm II, Poslednji nemački imperator i kralj Prusije

- Helmuth Johann Ludwig von Moltke, Šef Generalnog štaba Nemačke

- Alfred von Tirpitz, Veliki admiral, Državni sekretar Generalnog štaba nemačke mornarice

Statdschloss in Berlin, 1914, pred atentat u Sarajevu. Wilhelm otvara šampanjac. Sunce prosipa svoje tečno zlato.

Wilhelm	Kao što smo i znali, Rusija nije spremna za rat. Rusija Nikolaja II je izuzetno loše organizovana i korumpirana država. Veruje u mit o svojoj nepobedivosti, iako je doživela brojne poraze. Ruski "parni valjak", slabo opremljena vojska od milion i po vojnika i tri miliona rezervista, postoji samo na papiru. Neće se usuditi takvi da udju u rat. Ako naši vojnici i krenu na njih, vratiće se pre nego što opadne lišće. Živela nepokolebljiva nibelunška vernost! Zahvatićemo duboko u bunar nemačkih bajki. To je stari put, naša mistika i naš nemački barok, Klopstock i Herder, Goethe i Schiller, Kant i Fichte, Bach, Beethoven, Wagner! Vivat! *[Nazdravljaju]*
Moltke Tirpitz	Veličanstvo je svetsko čudo strateške dalekovidosti! Činjenica je da Rusi nisu spremni. I neće biti sve do 1916. S druge strane "Teorija rizične flote", da će naša flota, iako ne više upola slabija od engleske, odvratiti Britance od pokušaja pomorske blokade u Severnom moru - i dalje je samo ono što je i bila: "rizična teorija". Ako Britanci to ipak urade, uloga naše mornarice biće tužna. Ne može se sakriti grad što leži na gori.
Moltke	Neka Bog kazni Englesku! Nikad nisam sumnjao da će Britanci učestvovati u konfliktu. Britanska sebična politika se nije promenila, von Tirpitz. Oni se već dugo pripremaju za rat. Mada, ni mi nismo sedeli skrštenih ruku. Uostalom, rat je neizbežan, svi su vezani klauzulama. I biće gori nego što iko može da zamisli. I neće biti kratak. Razumem i brigu o konsekvencama

Wilhelm	koje će on doneti. Vi, von Moltke, potcenjujete moralne snage, koje rat pokreću! Takve crne misli ne priliče ovom blistavom danu. Krajnje je vreme da dodje do poleta duša! Nema mesta nervozi, ni bolesnoj zabrinutosti! Vreme je za ozbiljnost i ponosno dostojanstvo! Sjaj antičke veličine osvetljava naše doba! Imamo punu podršku naroda. Lepo je govorio Bismarck: "Naši ljudi su da ih poljubiš!" Narod je izvor u kojem možeš osvežiti dušu! Ljudi i inače nemaju šta drugo da rade. Ja sve merim pretrpljenim strahom i sramotom. Imam svoju skalu. Po njoj i naplaćujem. Posle ovog juna više nema natrag. Strah se digao kao laki vetar preko mora. Epoha se opet slama. Kakva tugovanka! Više nema kriterijuma za stvarnost. Rat može da počne. Ako i bude zločina, biće to sveti zločin! Nemačka više neće patiti od kompleksa mladjeg deteta. Sve će se odvijati kao u dobro uvežbanom pozorišnom komadu. I nemojte odmah da bečite oči kad neki general izgubi nekih osamdeset hiljada vojnika! Bitke nisu bitke, ako nisu bogate gubicima! Već na ovom svetu obećavam vam pobedu nad neprijateljima. Obećavam vam da duša koja ovaj plan bude poštovala neće izgubiti. Gde drugi padnu, mi ćemo se dići! Gde ostali mrze, mi ćemo voleti! Gde svi umiru, mi ćemo živeti! Nemac nema nikakvu drugu čežnju osim da ostane u svojoj zemlji i da se pošteno hrani od svojih kolonija. To moramo celom svetu jednom zauvek da utvimo u glavu. Vladanje palatama i velikim granicama, to je ono što je pred nama. Glavna je stvar da se naši ljudi dobro bore, ostalo će doći samo po sebi. A britanska zavist, francuska želja za osvetom i ruska grabežljivost - eto odgovora ko je kriv za rat! Ali, ruka božja stvara novi svet i pravi delotvorna čuda. *[Ispiju šampanjac]*
Wilhelm	Ne smemo dozvoliti da matori Franz Joseph poklekne u poslednji tren i padne u carstvo intimnih apsurda. Neka iskoristi dogadjaje koji su pred vratima da ostvari svoju staru nameru pokoravanja drčnih Slovena. Srpski nacionalizam i ekspanzionizam mu se sasvim lepo namestio. Kod Srba je sekira deo nameštaja. Previše su imali uspeha u Balkanskim ratovima. Beč mora da iskoristi svoju zlatnu šansu. Naravno, dobiće

	momentalno našu bezuslovnu podršku. Blanko ček im je već odavno uručen! Sposobnost južnjaka da se oduševljavaju mora da usmerava i reguliše nemačka ozbiljnost. Biće ultimatuma kao pleve ovoga leta. A Britanci možda ipak odustanu i ostanu izvan sukoba. Ko zna? Čitao sam u današnjim novinama da u Downing Streetu nema kupatila. Dakle, šta kažete! To sasvim liči na njih!
Moltke	Dobro, ali to ne znači da se nisu kupali stotinu godina.
Wilhelm	Kako? Meni se čini da ste vi skeptik! Engleska vladajuća klasa, to su sve sami masoni sasvim inficirani Judom.
Moltke	Najusrdnije hvala na audijenciji, ekselencijo. Sluga ponizni, ekselencijo!

Beč 2

DRAMATIS PERSONAE
- Franz Joseph I of Austria, Imperator Austrije i Apostolski kralj Madjarske

- Franz Ferdinand of Austria, Nadvojvoda austrijski, Austro-ugarski i kraljevski princ Madjarski

- Count Leopold Berthold, Anton Johann Sigismund Josef Korsinus Ferdinand, Ministar spoljnih poslova Austrije i bivši ambasador u Rusiji

Hofburg, Beč, 1914, pred atentat u Sarajevu. Berthold otvara šampanjac. Sunce prosipa svoje tečno zlato.

Berthold	No, prestonasledniče, želim od srca srećan i ugodan put u Sarajevo! Šteta da nećete imati vremena za lov u bosanskim šumama. Priča se da je divljač tamo izuzetna!
F Ferdinand	Zaista? Može biti, može biti. Guverner Potiorek nije ostavio nimalo slobodnog vremena svom Generalnom vojnom inspektoru. Vojni manevri, pokoji govor, i to bi bilo sve! Nadam se da neće bacati bombe na mene! Ovaj šampanjac je sasvim korektan. Vivat! *[Nazdravljaju]*
Berthold	Nije madjarski, možda zato... Francuski, klasična Brut metoda!
F Ferdinand	Ovaj razgovor je završen, zar ne? *[Nakloni se i izadje]*
Franz Joseph	Strah me je, grofe Berthold.
Berthold	Nema hrabrosti bez straha. Budući pokojni ljubimac! Od ovog istorijskog trenutka više se nećemo videti.
Franz Joseph	Bog da mu dušu prosti, neka ga djavo odnese!
Berthold	Jedno oko će vam biti vlažno, drugo vedro. Ne više od šest žandarma za Sarajevo, javljam pokorno. Ostali su nam potrebni za Beograd.
Franz Joseph	Ali, on ih ima više dok šeta kroz Beč!
Berthold	Za svet će, nota bene, ostati da je on bio u božjim rukama, nije se moglo sprečiti. Mnoge će čuditi da najmoćniji čovek monarhije nije mogao da sprovede

veću zaštitu za putovanje, medjutim moćnik kojeg više nema - nema uticaja. Jedan moćnik može sve, samo ne može sprečiti da bude ubijen. Ali kazniti kada se već jednom dogodilo - pitanje je prestiža! Biće to pogreb prve klase! I biće to ultimatum kakav još nije postavljen u modernom dobu. Tu onda mora biti zadovoljštine, to će uvideti svako dete. Mi ćemo biti naravno za mir, ali ne za mir po svaku cenu. Lagaćemo do poslednjeg čoveka. Da li ćemo se tako i boriti, to je drugo pitanje. Anonimnost je pola dobročinstva, to je posao diplomatije. Ali, samo tiho! Samo tiho! Vojnicima prepuštam ostalo! Malo će se uzburkati strasti, konačno! Treba pripremiti sve da se u Poštanskoj štedionici odmah donese odluka o finansijskoj potpori za rat. I obavezno pozvati dvorskog fotografa, da napravi jedan lep snimak kako je ekselencija zadubjena u proučavanje geografske karte Balkana. Onako diskretno! Uvek diskretno! Neusiljeno i odvažno! Da, to bi bilo prima! Ne bi bilo na odmet i po koje spretno novinarsko pero, pod hitno. Treba uspostaviti razumljivu vezu izmedju jezika i rata. Praktična bajka, poetsko sredstvo. Onda možemo pouzdano računati na duhovni zanos. Ideali donose pročišćenje narodu. Ne bi bilo lepo da ovo veliko vreme zatekne nekakvo malo pokoljenje. U ovom velikom vremenu svako sitničarenje je isključeno. Čovek, nota bene, ne sme dozvoliti da ga obuzme otrov pacifizma. Ratovi su blagoslov za ideale! Mirnodopska vremena su opasna vremena! Ratovi su procesi pročišćavanja i čišćenja, to su zasejana polja vrline i način budjenja heroja. Čast otadžbine mora značiti sve! Naša savest je čista! To je pravi austrijski realissimum! Ovo će biti rat u koji je naša otadžbina uvučena. Odbrambeni rat! Mada mi to zvuči kao da moramo da se izvinjavamo. Ali, svi će dobiti krst na grudima!

Franz Joseph Ja ga nosim na ledjima! Niko ozbiljan u svetu neće misliti kako relativno vojno slaba Austro-Ugarska nastupa sama. A Kajzer pritiska kao da je kraj sveta! Navalio je kao mutav! Srbija mora umreti, htela ili ne htela! Bla, bla, bla! Nema veze što mladobosanci uopšte nisu velikosrbi, već idealisti koji se izjašnjavaju

	kao Jugosloveni, ili Srbohrvati, inspirisani panslovenskim i levičarskim idejama. Velika se nesreća sprema. Bojim se da će oni koji danas kliču sutra plakati. Možda još ima vremena za strategijsko povlačenje. Strategijsko povlačenje je uvek uspeh.
Berthold	Vaše Carsko i Kraljevsko Veličanstvo takoreći huška za mir! Dozvolite, ali čast otadžbine mora značiti sve! Marš princa Eugena ponovo odjekuje! Kakva imperijalna panorama! Svakom čoveku je potrebno malo borbe i oluje. Sa Srbijom ćemo pevajući izaći na kraj. Konačno će platiti za sve svoje zavereničke akcije protiv Monarhije. Sve ostalo će ići automatski. More će svetla zasjati! Nego, šta kažete za našu diplomatiju? Za taj posao je potrebna odvažnost! Jedan pogodak za drugim! Mi nismo započeli rat, mi smo ga samo želeli! Još samo da ne spreče ultimatum! Bićemo takoreći primorani da dopustimo da nas napadnu. Mlada Bosna, Mlada Turska, Mlada Italija, Mlada Poljska, sve to ima samo jedan cilj: da unište multinacionalne monarhije! Pa zar bi trebalo da se ženiramo? Oh! Kakav divan rat! Naša dela nam otvaraju put i naš cilj je polazište slave! Austrija će uskrsnuti kao falanga iz svetskog požara! Mit o Austriji će živeti!
Franz Joseph	Mitovi su javni snovi, snovi su privatni mitovi. A sada svi jedva čekaju da opašu sablju! Habzburg kao Damoklov mač lebdi nad svetskim mirom! Strah me je. Antihrist jeblizu. Sanjao sam noćas kapitulaciju na kopnu, moru i u vazduhu! I sanjao sam da je general Geza von Lakati Nemesfalva et Kutyavilag Faluszeg imao neslavno povlačenje iz Galicije; da je opet na pogrešnom mestu viknuo ura, a onda je došao da mi objašnjava kako se jednostavno otkačio od neprijatelja i samo ga vuče za sobom! Pridobili su me za svetski rat! Sve sam dobro promislio ali, eto, ne mogu drugačije! Bez ikakvog razloga milione ljudi pretvaram u leševe i bogalje. Veliki Bože, ne dozvoli da budem svedok! Ne dozvoli, za ljubav blagoslovene krvi Isusove! Večnost je već načeta! Izgoreli smo! Ko je kriv, draga domovino?
Berthold	Najusrdnije hvala na audijenciji, ekselencijo! Sluga

ponizni, ekselencijo!

Beograd 2

DRAMATIS PERSONAE
- Alexander Karadjordjević, Princ prestolonaslednik Kraljevine Srbije, Regent u Srbiji

- Dragutin Dimitrijević Apis, , Potpukovnik Srpske armije, vodeći član tajne vojne grupe Crna ruka, šef Obaveštajnog odeljenja u Ministarstvu rata

- Vojislav Tankosić, major u Srpskoj armiji, četnički vojvoda, jedan od osnivača tajne vojne grupe Crna ruka

Beograd, ušće Save i Dunava, 1914, pred atentat u Sarajevu. Tankosić otvara šampanjac. Aleksandar pije čaj. Sunce rasipa svoje tečno zlato.

Tankosić Eno ga crno-žuti barjak! Neka nas gledaju Austrijanci preko reke kako nazdravljamo! Imaju jake sprave! Izvinjavam se, ekselencijo, mogu prilično jasno da vide kako češem dupe!

Aleksandar	Prestanite s nepristojnim lakrdijama, zaboga! Dosta ste ih već učinili. Nema nikakvog razloga za nazdravljanje. Ako se dogodi još bilo kakva glupost, moja će vlada morati da izlazi u susret austro-ugarskoj do krajnjih granica popustljivosti. *[Tankosić ponudi šampanjac Aleksandru i Apisu. Aleksandar odbije]*
Aleksandar	Hvala. Hoćete li vi čaj možda?
Tankosić	Ne, niti sada, niti ikada!
Apis	Živela Srbija! *[Nazdravljaju]*
Tankosić	Pravda će pobediti!
Aleksandar	Ako tražite pravdu, onda živite u pogrešnom stoleću.
Tankosić	Ne tražim ja ništa, osim da njihova vlada i njihove diplomate gacaju kroz more krvi i suza, neka im je proklet porod! Vidite li onu karaulu tamo? Prva stvar koju ću uraditi prve noći kada se zapuca - je da odem tamo sa svojim četnicima, razoružam i skinem stražare, gologuze ih pošaljem u Zemun, i istaknem srpsku zastavu! A posle se u austrijskim uniformama vratim preko reke u Beograd, sednem u "Zlatnu morunu" i naručim piće za celu kafanu! A zatim ću da nadjem i izbatinam ministre koji će već prve noći pokušati da izbegnu iz grada i stvore paniku u narodu. *[Pesnicom preti Austro-Ugarskoj preko reke]*
Tankosić	Nadmene hijene, kuvaću čorbu na vašem požaru! Krvi ću vam se napiti! A onim Srbima iz Bosne koje budem uhvatio u austrijskoj uniformi, uši ću lično poodsecati, turskoga im krsta!
Apis	Molim Regenta da ne obraća pažnju na Tankosićevo ponašanje. Lirska zver, takoreći! Pomalo udaren, ali izrazito simpatičan! Uprkos djavolu i smrti i kricima naših neprijatelja.
Aleksandar	Niste ni vi ništa bolji, potpukovniče Dimitrijević! Načinili ste ogroman korak u pogrešnom smeru, tako tipično srpski! Oduvek smo bili neuki prema sudbini. Zar mislite, potpukovniče, da je širenje vaše mreže po Bosni, Austrijancima ostalo nevidljivo? Kao da oni ne znaju šta ste sve galamili u "Zlatnoj moruni!" O ponašanju majora Tankosića da i ne govorim! Kako, recimo, puca u jabuke na ramenima svojih vojnika! Crna ruka nimalo nije pomogla državnoj politici, u ovom

	slučaju. Preneo sam vam odavno da su Rusi molili da sad ništa ne započinjete. Niste hteli da slušate. A sad smo zaprečeni ovom užasnom situacijom! Samo da znate da je predsednik vlade, gospodin Pašić, obavestio Bečki dvor da se sprema atentat. Austro-Ugarska je dobila pravo, još na Berlinskom kongresu, da okupira Bosnu na trideset godina! A Rusija se još pre toga obavezala da neće imati ništa protiv austrijske aneksije Bosne, nakon isteka tog perioda. Svidelo se to vama ili ne - tako je! Vaša crnorukaška kontrola Mlade Bosne, vaše "Ujedinjenje ili smrt", moglo je malo da sačeka sa tom jeftinom patriotiotskom frazeologijom! Ko će uopšte poverovati da zvanična Srbija nije u tome učestvovala? Srbija je svakojake zulume činila u Balkanskim ratovima, niko to ne zna bolje od vas. Mislite li da je to zaboravljeno? Sa jednim narodom je gotovo kada mrtve fraze vuče za sobom tamo gde ponovo oživljava njihov sadržaj. To je dokaz da taj narod više ne doživljava.
Apis	Poznato vam je da sam poslao svog oficira u Bosnu da zaustavi stvar. Odbijen je, vaše kraljevsko visočanstvo. Dok, u isto vreme, Austro-Ugarska Pašićevo upozorenje nije ozbiljno shvatila. Nije htela. Šta vam to govori, vaše kraljevsko visočanstvo?
Aleksandar	Da će biti rata, potpukovniče. Da će biti strašnog rata. Ne znate vi ništa o svetskoj istoriji.
Tankosić	Svetska istorija se kod nas pojavljuje dva puta dnevno, vaše kraljevsko visočanstvo. Dakle, isuviše često da bi obezbedila potreban autoritet. Medjutim, mnogo neprijatelja, mnogo časti! Smrt nam nije strana! Moraću opet da činim čuda od junaštva. Kuća u kojoj živim nalazi se tačno preko puta nemačkog poslanstva. Prvo ću njih da zapalim. A moj poslednji poklič u sledećem ratu će biti: Za mnom ko hoće da pogine!
Aleksandar	Nemam reči. To bi nam zaista pomoglo. Baš kao i činjenica da ste svojevremeno mladom britanskom dopisniku Winstonu Churchillu, nezadovoljni njegovim izveštavanjem iz Srbije, nalupali šamare u kafani. Pa je pod policijskom pratnjom ispraćen na beogradsku železničku stanicu. A moralo je i da se sastavlja zvanično izvinjenje. E, pa on je sada Prvi lord u Admiralitetu! I ko zna šta će još postati?

Tankosić	Može da bude šta hoće, briga me! K'o što je i njega, uostalom.
Apis	Najusrdnije hvala na audijenciji, vaše kraljevsko visočanstvo!

Sarajevo

DRAMATIS PERSONAE
- Gavrilo Princip, pripadnik južnoslovenske tajne organizacije Mlada Bosna, atentator na Franza Ferdinanda

Sarajevo, 28. juni 1914. Potpuni mrak. Dva pucnja.

Bilo gde u Evropi

DRAMATIS PERSONAE
- Kolporter

Kolporter prodaje novine na ulici, 28. juni - 12. avgust 1914.

KOLPORTER: Prestolonaslednik i supruga ubijeni! Vanredno izdanje! Zaverenici uhapšeni! Vanredno izdanje! Osećanje duboke potresenosti! Nezadovoljstvo u Engleskoj! Očajanje u Rusiji! Potištenost u Italiji! Izgubljenost u Belgiji! Demoralizacija u Srbiji! Defetizam u Crnoj Gori! Ljutnja u Austriji! Pretnje u Nemačkoj! Vanredno izdanje! Vanredno izdanje! Austro-Ugarska objavila rat Srbiji! Nemačka objavila rat Rusiji! Nemačka objavila rat Francuskoj! Nemačka objavila rat Belgiji! Velika Britanija objavila rat Nemačkoj! Crna Gora objavila rat Austro-Ugarskoj! Austro-Ugarska objavila rat Rusiji! Srbija objavila rat Nemačkoj! Crna Gora objavila rat Nemačkoj! Francuska objavila rat Austro-Ugarskoj! Britanija objavila rat Austro-Ugarskoj! Vanredno izdanje! Rusija nikome nije objavila rat! Vanredno izdanje! Crna Gora objavila rat svima! Vanredno izdanje! Velikoj Britaniji niko nije objavio rat! Velika Britanija objavila rat svima! Vanredno izdanje!

Finale - London 2

DRAMATIS PERSONAE

- Optimista 2

- Zanovetalo 2

High-tech kancelarija u centru Londona. Godina 2014. Optimista i Zanovetalo sede, svaki za svojim stolom, jedan preko puta drugog. Ne gledaju jedan drugog, nego zure u svoje kompjutere.

Zanovetalo	CNN je zabrinut jer se kašlje u Ukrajini. Molim da se na mene ne računa u grupi zabrinutih. Ta TV stanica je hronično zabrinuta za sudbinu čitavog sveta. Iz sata u sat zasipaju me informacijama o zabrinutosti zbog eventualne podele Ukrajine. Zašto je svojevremeno otcepljenje Ukrajine, sve sa sovjetskim nuklearnim bojevim glavama, bilo veselo i opuštajuće, a ovo sada izaziva formulu zabrinutosti? Nije li to logika nedorečenosti?
Optimista	Tamo je neophodna humanitarna intervencija!
Zanovetalo	Bilo bi zgodno pomoći stanovništvu Krima, ali problem

	je u tome što ono ne traži pomoć! Ovde ne traži situacija humanitarnu intervenciju, ovde humanitarna intervencija traži situaciju, a situacije nema! A bez te floskule o humanitarnoj intervenciji, rat postaje direktni naturalistički rat za interese, za resurse, za kontrolu i moć. Aplaudiralo se kada se raspadao Sovjetski savez, kada se raspadala Čehoslovačka, kada se raspadala Jugoslavija. Taj patos padajućih granica je tada bio dobar, a sada kada se raspada Ukrajina, još jedna nehomogena država, to je odjednom zabrinjavajuća stvar! Po kom kriterijumu je neko padanje granica loše, a neko dobro? Kad Zapad bombarduje Srbiju - Milosrdni andjeo, kad Rusi zauzmu Krim - Nemilosrdni andjeo! Kako se to zapadna politička misao našla u tako šizofrenoj situaciji političke iskompromisanosti? Gde se podizanju granica treba radovati, a gde tugovati? Putin nije toliko simpatičan predsednik kao urugvajski, ali uputio je ključno pitanje demokratskom svetu.
Optimista	A koje to?
Zanovetalo	Pitao ih je zašto podržavaju demonstracije u Kijevu, a u Sarajevu ne.
Optimista	A oni?
Zanovetalo	A oni nisu znali odgovor. Pa je onda postavio još jedno pitanje.
Optimista	A koje to?
Zanovetalo	Kako to da podržavaju revolucionarnu vladu u Kijevu, a ne i revolucionarnu vladu na Krimu? Ili, da vam prevedem na engleski, kako to da je referendum na Falklandima prihvatljiv, a referendum na Krimu nije?
Optimista	A oni opet nisu znali odgovor?
Zanovetalo	Kako ste samo pogodili! Ali, onoliko koliko ne treba verovati Zapadu kada priča o demokratiji, toliko isto ne treba verovati Rusiji kada priča o idealima.
Optimista	Poštedite me vaših modernih zanovetanja! Ceremonija je bila divna! Sto godina je prošlo! Svi se danas sećaju palih heroja! Odaju im počast! Kako je to lepo! I kako je

Zanovetalo	to uzbudljivo! I kako je to samo dostojanstveno! Nikakva raskoš, samo tiha tuga! Da. Sve vrvi od zvezda i korifeja. Vaše optimističko prisustvo se samo po sebi razumevalo. Tmurno jutro. Molitve na vojnom groblju uvek dobro prolaze. Situacija palih heroja je zaista bila izuzetna. Ispaštali su zbog nepoznate krivice. Otrov, noć i otadžbina. Samo hrabro napred! Na Somu! Pobeda je naša! Samo napred! Idite! Idite! Svi ćete da umrete i ponašajte se shodno tome! Bog je s vama, pucajte revnosno u neprijatelja! Vi ste držali položaje, lepi moji. Ispred vas neprijatelj, iza vas otadzbina. Ko je gori? A iznad večite zvezde. Blaženi zaborav pred smrt. Trebalo je ovom prilikom da podele lakrimarijume političarima, da suze koje danas prolivaju za ondašnjim žrtvama, sačuvaju za neki sledeći rat. Svi oni su umetnici laži, oni sami ne veruju u nju, ali žele da je čuju, jer im laž jasnije kazuje šta osećaju. Zar samoprolivena krv nije samo rubin, lažni dijamant, prava suza, ukras koji pozajmljuje Judino nakaradno lice? Od svega je ostala samo žanr slika: gipka i sjajna mladost nabijena silnom energijom plamti od revnosti i osećanja važnosti, od osećanja pripadnosti nebeskom narodu, novoj i snažnoj rasi, ispunjenoj voljom. Oči skamenjene ispod kacige, oči što šire stravu, trijumf fantastične groze, budući neimari na razorenim temeljima sveta. Svakom svoje. Heroju grob. Hteo je da oslobodi svet, a on se oslobodio njega. I onda odjednom, mir, tišina, muk. Vije se dim nad bojištem, među stablima leluljaju senke, zalazi krvavo sunce. U štab stiže flaša pravog šampanjca i konzerva pravog kavijara. Reš kifle i šareno cveće, rotkvice i damastni čaršav. Takvih kontrasta ima samo na frontu.
Optimista	Kako samo preterujete! Svako vreme ima svoj rat.
Zanovetalo	Svako vreme ima svoju kugu. Svaka epoha ima epidemiju kakvu zaslužuje. A ova je bila takva da je možda, po prvi put od vremena stvaranja sveta, djavo uzviknuo: dodjavola! I to sve zbog nekoliko nemaštovitih nitkova! Sto godina je prošlo! A akademska koplja se još lome oko toga ko je odgovorni urednik, ko je Ares, a ko Merkur svetskog rata? Jedni krive Nemačku, koja je imala moć da zaustavi ulazak u katastrofu, povlačenjem podrške Austriji za napad na

Srbiju. Kažu da ni Rusija nije želela rat, barem ne odmah. A ni Srbija, iscrpljena Balkanskim ratovima. Drugi kažu da je upravo Srbija kriva, jer su njeni nacionalizam i ekspanzionizam bili najdublje remetilačke sile, što se najviše vidi preko podrške zvaničnog Beograda Crnoj ruci. Treći opet kažu da su austrougarski, nemački i ruski vojni sokolovi krivci za svetski konflikt. Neki tvrde da je zakazala diplomatija. Nemački autori danas optužuju i Britaniju, izmedju ostalih. Izdvaja se naučni rad u kojem se tvrdi da je Princip Jevrejin i mason. Gabrijel, a ne Gavrilo! Originalno, zar ne! Taj autor zaista ima mašte, i duše, i duha, i mišljenje! Mazel tov! Jedini rezultat, medjutim, izgleda da su bili milioni tona potonulog duha. Grmljavina je zatim prestala da tutnji i ne znamo šta je od nas želela. U britanskoj vojsci je bilo dvesta pedeset hiljada maloletnih lica. Sidney Lewis je imao samo 12 godina kada je, opijen patriotizmom, rasporedjen u mitraljesku jedinicu na Somi. I samo se nadam da pred Strašnim sudom zaista nema ošljarenja. I da se tamo ne može za sebe srediti stvar, kako je to već naviknuto. I želim vam reći da je bogougodnije odati visočanstvu smrti počast na grobnicama mladića i muškaraca, majki i dece koji su umrli od metka ili gladi, nego na grobovima u kojima počivaju oni koji su sve to zrelo promislili i jednim potezom pera prouzrokovali. Onih koji ne razlikuju ručnu granatu od gomilice izmeta! Našu sudbinu odredio je demon osrednjosti. Gospodari krvi ! Mediokriteti i njihova učena neznanja! A modulacije besne i zvekeću kroz vreme. Kulminiraju u zlokobne radnje i nove partije remija - u istinsku perspektivu pogrešnog života. Potpuno u skladu sa satanskom sudbinom, koja nas od malih činjenica vodi do velike tragedije.

Optimista   Zanemeću! Čoveku se para srce, kad čuje kako govorite.

Zanovetalo   Šta ćete, rat pretvara život u dečiju sobu, u kojoj je onaj drugi uvek prvi počeo i u kojoj se jedan hvali zločinom koji drugom prebacuje. Neverovatne rečenice čije bezumlje trajno odzvanja doslovno su izgovarane, najneverovatnija dela zaista su se dogodila. A ja vam kažem: bagra je jednostavno pravila ujdurmu! Vi ste

	optimista i jednostavno ne želite da vidite ljude koji jedu govna. Živele svinje, njihovo je carstvo nebesko!
Optimista	Popravljač sveta! - velika stvar! Vi ste oduvek bili pesimista u vezi s ratom! Samo vi ostanite u svom ćošku i zanovetajte! Kakva malodušnost! Svaki rat završava mirom. Zar ne vidite da je zato danas nastupilo veliko doba?
Zanovetalo	Poznavao sam ga dok je još bilo malo, i opet će takvo postati. Kakva gigantska sićušnost! Svetski rat je bio rezultat realtivno male medjunarodne krize, pogrešnih procena, straha od gubitka prestiža i tvrdoglave posvećenosti veoma složenom sistemu vojnih zabluda i političkih savezništava. Bio je to rat iluzija. Ultimatum Srbiji je bio takav da je unapred bilo jasno da ga neće prihvatiti. Nijedna zemlja na svetu ga ne bi mogla prihvatiti. Čak i da ga je prihvatila, nikakav oblik prihvatanja, ma kako bedan bio, ne bi zadovoljio agresora. I to zato jer se nekima činilo da je trenutak savršen! A onda je to neko nazvao promišljenom politikom. Sto godina je prošlo, optimisto, a još ne znamo ko je kriv. Zaboravljena noć. Ne mogu čak ni oko broja žrtava da se slože. Ne znamo ni bilans krvi. Vreme ništa ne leči, vreme je ubica. Otadžbini, tom pozivaru koji još uvek raspolaže najvećom sugestijom; otadžbini - to jest komisiji strvodera i svinja - trebalo je da uskrate svoje telo i svoju dušu. Trebalo je da svi učine upravo to.
Optimista	Šta znači pojedinačna patnja? Isto tako malo i pojedinačni život! I zar patnja nije božija stvar? Čovekov pogled je uperen prema gore. Čovek ne živi samo od hleba!
Zanovetalo	Već mora da vodi ratove da ga ne bi imao.
Optimista	Šta ćete, tako je u ratu! Vama je važno samo da zanovetate! Ja jesam i ostajem optimista! Narodi kroz štetu postaju -
Zanovetalo	- glupi.
Optimista	Kad bi otadžbina mislila kao vi, lepo bi to izgledalo!
Zanovetalo	Otadžbina misli tako.
Optimista	Jutarnje svetlo na kraju uvek osvaja tamu! I život se oporavlja od mukotrpnih dela!
Zanovetalo	Od mukotrpnih dela jedne pohlepne civilizacije.
Optimista	Eto, sad opet zanovetate! Pohlepa je dobra. Obeležila

	je evoluciju čovečanstva. Ona je stvorila civilizaciju! Ona je u svim vidovima dobra!
Zanovetalo	Prava reč u pravo vreme! Reč jednog optimiste! Konačno se u nečemu slažemo. Da! I tako smo dobili pohlepnu civilizaciju, u kojoj pohlepa proizvodi ratove, u kojoj pohlepa proglašava mir, u kojoj pohlepa odredjuje čak i cenu spajalice na toj vašoj fascikli, koju držite na stolu. I u kojoj pohlepni šefovi pohlepnih država ne mogu biti pozvani na odgovornost zbog svog pohlepnog delovanja. Ali, mi smo naše tirane uvek nadoknadjivali od nas samih. I tada dodje kraj i ništa ne ostaje! Kyrie Eleison!
Optimista	Demokratija je pobedila, moliću lepo!
Zanovetalo	Vi zaista kažete sve, pa i još povrh toga! U društvima demokratskog sveta jedan procenat stanovništva drži pedeset procenata ukupnog bogatstva. Nemojte reći da ste zaista poverovali u tu demokratsku priču!
Optimista	Vama ništa nije sveto! Koju vi to ideju zastupate?
Zanovetalo	Kao zanovetalo sam obavezan da sve vidim crno. Zastupam, dakle, ideju da Bog nije stvorio čoveka kao potrošača ili proizvodjača, već kao čoveka. Da životna namirnica nije cilj života. Da život nije zasnovan na isključivosti i interesima privredjivanja. Da je čovek smešten u vreme da bi imao vremena, a ne da nogama stigne negde brže nego srcem. Kuda ideš, Evropo? Nisi se izlečila od svojih najopasnijih istina. Gori li opet na sve strane? Epoha se opet slama? Kakva tugovanka! Mislili smo da će nam se istorija - bez obzira koliko farsična, ponoviti u lepšem izdanju, barem spolja nalik na nešto drugo od tragedije. Nemačka je htela da bude imperijalna sila, što danas i jeste, i bez vojske. I opet je suviše mala da bi dominirala kontinentom i previše jaka da bi igrala sama; opet je poluhegemon. Austro-Ugarske nema, a bila je dobra država. Ispostavilo se, medjutim, da je njihov ultimatum bio prava glupost. Granica Srbije je, gle čuda, opet na Merdaru, tamo gde je vojvoda Tankosić započeo Prvi Balkanski rat, bez odobrenja nadležne komande. Nema više ni Jugoslavije, za koju su se borili mladobosanci, i koje je takodje bila dobra država. A Bosna danas u Sarajevu opet ima austrijskog guvernera, baš kao i pre sto godina. I sada, sto godina posle, opet su demonstracije

	po Bosni. Izgoreo je arhiv i dokazi o zločinima. I Bosna je još uvek ogledalo Evrope! Kao i Ukrajina! Po prvi put nakon rušenja Berlinskog zida kapitalizam oseća strah, njemu tako potreban, kako bi zauzdao svoj nezajažljivi apetit. Živela ravnoteža straha! Bez nje, ta ogromna kapitalistička usta proždiru i ono što ne mogu da svare. Odsustvo ideologije nadoknadjujemo ideologijom granica. Eto nas, vraćamo se na granice Berlinskog kongresa, što znači da su svetski ratovi dvadesetog veka, ne samo prvi, nego i drugi, vodjeni ama potpuno bez veze! Gde smo bili, Evropo- nigde! Šta smo radili, Evropo - ništa! Toliki mrtvi i iskasapljeni - a Bože moj! Rat je bio dečija igra u odnosu na mir koji je uspostavljen; delta ka velikoj vodi ludila. Posle rata još više rata i više patnji. Da li ste zadovoljni? Prepuštam vašem izvežbanom optimizmu da se opredeli.
Optimista	"Zadovoljan" nije nikakva reč! Nazovite to ljubavlju prema otadžbini, vi idealisti; mržnjom prema neprijatelju, vi nacionalisti; nazovite to sportom, vi savremeni ljudi; avanturom, vi romantičari; nazovite to nasladom snage, vi poznavaoci duše; poslednjim danima, vi zanovetala - ja to nazivam oslobodjenim čovečanstvom!
Zanovetalo	Kako to nazivate?
Optimista	Oslobodjenim čovečanstvom!

K R A J ?

Programme For Novi Sad.

Finger Trigger Bullet Gun

Written by Nenad Prokić

Translated by Mirka Jankovic

Performed by
Gerard Bell – Graeme Rose – Craig Stephens – Jack Trow

Costumes – Kay Wilton
Lighting – Simon Bond
Direction – James Yarker

Administrator – Rowena Wilding
Executive Producer – Roisin Caffrey

First performed as part of London International Festival of Theatre on 28th June, 2014 exactly 100 years after the assassination of Arch Duke Ferdinand.

Co-commissioned by LIFT and 14-18 Now, WW1 Centenary Art Commissions (supported by the National Lottery Through the Heritage Lottery Fund and Arts Council England).

Presented in Birmingham as part of BE Festival.

Thanks To:
LIFT, Birmingham Repertory Theatre
Professor Nebojsa Randjelovic University of Nis
Staff & students at Washwood Heath Academy
(who made the original dominos)
Gareth Nicholls (who performed in the original production)
Phil Holyman, and Charlotte Martin.

Biography:

Nenad Prokić is a Serbian Playwright based in Belgrade, where he is professor of Twentieth Century Drama at the University of Art. He was official playwright for the Yugoslav Drama theatre for a decade as well as the Slovenian National Theatre. It was as Director of the Belgrade International Festival of Theatre that he first met Stan's Cafe.

In 2003 Prokić founded the Liberal Democratic Party in Serbia and served two terms in the Serbian Parliament before resigning from the party and retiring from party politics in 2012.

Finger Trigger Bullet Gun, his first play in 25 years, was commissioned for After A War, London International Festival of Theatre's commemoration of the start of the First World War.

Stan's Cafe devise original theatre shows from their base in Birmingham, England and tour them around the world. For more information on Stan's Cafe please visit www.stanscafe.co.uk.

Blog Post For The Guardian.

The trick is to find the metaphor, a way in which a show's form can help articulate its content. The First World War is our most pressing challenge. Last year Serbian playwright/politician Nenad Prokić related an encounter he had with Karl Popper in which the philosopher, whilst conceding that a Serbian finger had pulled the trigger which started the First World War, asked "who put the bullet in that gun?"

When LIFT's *After A War* season gave us the opportunity to invite Prokić to answer Popper's question, our main role became to find the metaphoric device that best supports his text.

In Sarajevo a finger pulls a trigger and a bullet from a gun knocks down a man, that man falling starts a chain reaction of others falling, which spreads across Europe. This sequence is clearly crying out for a great toppling of dominoes. So our challenge moves on. Can we harness the tension of a stage covered in thousands of dominoes balanced ready to fall and deploy this to power a drama enacted on that stage? It seems worth trying.

The next challenge is logistical. How do we get hold of thousands of dominoes ripe for the toppling? We ask Washwood Heath Academy, one of our partner schools, they have a great technology department who agree to cut 'dominoes' from MDF as part of a topic day devoted to learning about the First World War. Students inscribe the dominoes with names of soldiers killed on the Somme, turning them into miniature gravestones before setting them up in the Sports Hall. 15,000 dominoes stand and most fall. We learn a lot about angles and loops, safety breaks, speed of construction and how difficult it is to stay accurate and precise when we are tired. I had hoped to learn more, but ensuring the students had a rewarding day drew focus from timing rates of fall and density of dominoes per square metre. Fall time will be key, Prokić has written text to be read through the fall. I suspect it will need to be cut back but I have no idea by how much.

Having addressed basic mechanics, aesthetics return as a concern. How do the actors and dominoes share the stage? Originally I imagined three actors plotting around a table whilst around them two further performers set up the dominoes; the two worlds would be separate but speak to each other. How dull and limiting.

Auditions provided a good opportunity to test some ideas. We called prospective actors in groups of three and tried them in different formats. Instead of a table we placed dominoes at the centre of the stage and suddenly this world made a lot more sense. I could imagine the dominoes as a map of Europe over which the protagonists stride and argue.

The striding is clearly going to be a challenge. We can't have the actors carefully tiptoeing their way between the dominoes. They have to be confident, arrogant even, but at the same time if any domino gets flicked it will fall and start a disastrous chain-reaction which will ruin the show. A fluffed line is soon smoothed over, misplaced sound or light cues are terrible but contained mistakes, a mistimed topple would be a total disaster. It will be a high wire act.

It is the tension of this high wire act that we are after, but we will have to be careful to control how this tension works. If audiences become too concerned about the dominoes pre-empting their cue and toppling early, then they will have their attention distracted from the script. We could find ourselves scuppered by our own staging device whatever happens.

I suspect this is a conundrum that can only be solved in the rehearsal room. Here I imagine the actors will shape where the dominoes can stand and the dominoes will determine how the actors must move. Sharing the stage with thousands of dominoes is a scary prospect but in my book it's probably only the scary things that are worth doing at all.

James Yarker, 30th May, 2014

Nenad's Challenge

A message sent from Artistic Director James Yarker to Playwright Nenad Prokić. Much of what follows did not then happen!

Following our discussion in the Library of Birmingham these are my reflections on how we could move things forward.

For me the dominos are key. The main structuring device is the tension of the dominoes being set up ready for a fall. The audience know it is inevitable, that the dominoes will fall, the only questions are when they will fall, who will trigger the fall and whether any of them will be left standing. Anything we want to 'say' with our structuring should be said through the metaphor of the dominoes. I don't think it is very helpful to think too much about existing structures or theatrical forms; we are making something new.

This is a chamber piece. It is probably not acted on a stage but in a room with the audience all around it. I don't think there should be any action except the setting up of the dominos and the three people talking around the table. Maybe someone can stand up and back down before returning to the table but I imagine the table floating in a world of dominoes – three powerful men sitting on a vast map of Europe. There are no big stage pictures beyond this, this will give us enough to work with.

I am excited by the possibility of there being two modes of writing in the piece. The first is historic dialogue, taut and dramatic, all set in the build-up to the assassination, the figure pulling the trigger / toppling the first dominoe. The second is a more contemporary voice, monologue descriptions of living with war in Belgrade. I suggest the first is carefully translated and the second transcribed from your speech with your spoken grammar and word choices intact.

The actors around the table could play figures from the secret Berlin meeting throughout, or switch between other groups of three people talking round a table. The people setting up the dominos can be just functionaries whose job it is to set up the dominos. Once the convention is established that the actors around the table speak as fictional characters and those setting up the dominos are not acting but silently carrying out a real task, it would then come as a surprise if we chose to let these actors speak and speak as characters. It would become a 'coup de theatre' if one of them assumes the character of Princip to topple the first domino.

Does this sound possible? My feeling is we should create this piece as a tennis match, passing material back and forth between us many times.

James Yarker 16th December, 2013

Nenad's Answers

For those of us who don't know your previous plays, how does this piece compare with those that came before?

Finger Trigger Bullet Gun is different. James, in awe before the horrific bloodbath of the First World War, did not want any music in the production. In the same vein I did not want to use dramaturgical tricks or any smart rhythms to sweeten something that cannot and should not be sweetened. This is not a skilfully edited theatre treat. It was hard on everyone; me to write it, the translator to translate it, James to direct it, actors to play it and the spectators to watch it. It is in its essence a negative theatre, like Brecht's, but without songs.

Beyond historical exposition there is a rage and despair within this play which I find very powerful. I'm interested in how much (if at all) you drew on personal experiences?

I strongly believed that I would belong to the first modern generation which, in this tiny speck of the globe where I come from, would not live to see a war. I thought that history, no matter how farcical it may be, would be repeated in a nicer version, as something other than tragedy - on the outside at least. Needless to say, I was wrong. The future becomes less predictable with every passing day.

The play has a tight formal structure, did you find this constricting in your writing difficult or useful?

I feel tremendously responsible for every word written, quite excessively so. All my structures are like that, as if somebody at CERN had written them. I cannot resist this desire for some kind of order, for the reduction to the essential, for absolute symmetry. We are attracted by the womb like comfort of dogmas, while in fact we fall in love with the excitement of disorder. What you don't know is much more relevant than that do know. The unexpected is what kindles our fire. And this conflict is what tears me apart.

Finger Trigger Bullet Gun was written shortly after you left Serbian party politics, was it informed by your time in parliament?

Sure it was. When I stepped into that political madhouse I regretted it but it also cleared my vision because I glimpsed the very bottom of hell and it looks much worse there than those who have not set foot there would think. Politics is the basest form of humanity but this is precisely how the world is woven, so it was a valuable exercise, it prevents me being lulled into believing that our state of affairs is not all that bad, it is. Nobody thinks well of the Brexit phenomenon, but the real truth about Brexit is undoubtedly much worse than the worst you can imagine. Only art can, in a way, save us from politics. It has no master or it is not art.

Tell us a little about the play's translation and how that process worked.

I was fortunate to meet Mrs. Mirka Jankovic in my early days in theatre. She is well-read and a very good translator. Her translations always teach me something new about what I have written. I give her my text and trust her absolutely and, I'd say, she trusts me too. Nothing bears fruit in this world without a rapport.

In the final section you bring in the political crisis in Crimea at what point did that become part of your plan?

It's simple: former political manipulations can be explained by the present ones because they are identical; just as political crimes return in this recycled history as if they have never happened before and as if we have never suffered from them before. Political criminals are extremely unimaginative but they make up for this lack of imagination with monstrous cheek.

Would you ever consider writing a play directly about the break up of Yugoslavia and the horrific drama this precipitated?

All my plays are about Yugoslavia, even the one about Dante. About transient things one should write in a non-transient manner. Some succeed, some do not.

March 2019

About the illustration and design

The illustrations for the covers of these books were undertaken by students at Birmingham City University as the final module of their first-year illustration course during the Spring/Summer of 2018. The images were developed through workshops using variations of the theatre-devising methods employed by Stan's Cafe but adapted and applied to the making of visual work. The resulting work was shown in the pop-up exhibition *The Something Of Somebody Something* at Stan's Cafe's venue @AE Harris in May 2018.

The design concept of the books was produced by final year Graphic Design student Aimee Chapman. These were then further developed for print in a collaborative process between Stan's Cafe and the University's Innovation Product Support Service (IPSS) which involved helping the company to select appropriate DTP software, undertaking training and selecting a suitable print on demand service.

Gareth Courage
Lecturer in Illustration
Birmingham City University

www.ingramcontent.com/pod-product-compliance
Lightning Source LLC
Chambersburg PA
CBHW071755080526
44588CB00013B/2241